Durham
Pennines and
Tyne & Wear

C000283822

WALKS

Compiled by
Brian Conduit
and John Brooks

Margaret & Tessa.
0191- 2365800.

ARROLD

Ordnance
Survey

Acknowledgements
We would like to thank Mike Ogden and Simon Hodgson of
Durham County Council Environment Department for their
help in preparing the text and maps. Our thanks also for the
valuable advice and numerous useful leaflets that we
obtained from the various tourist information centres
throughout the area.

Text: Brian Conduit, John Brooks
Photography: Brian Conduit, John Brooks
Editor: Geoffrey Sutton
Designers: Brian Skinner, Doug Whitworth

Series Consultant: Brian Conduit

Jarrold Publishing   ISBN 0-7117-1098-8

While every care has been taken to ensure the accuracy of
the route directions, the publishers cannot accept
responsibility for errors or omissions, or for changes in
details given. The countryside is not static: hedges and
fences can be removed, field boundaries can be altered,
footpaths can be rerouted and changes in ownership can
result in the closure or diversion of some concessionary
paths. Also, paths that are easy and pleasant for walking in
fine conditions may become slippery, muddy and difficult in
wet weather, while stepping-stones across rivers and streams
may become impassable.
    If you find an inaccuracy in either the text or maps, please
write to Jarrold Publishing at the address below.

First published 2000
by Jarrold Publishing

Printed in Belgium
by Proost NV, Turnhout 1/00

Jarrold Publishing
Whitefriars, Norwich NR3 1TR

Front cover: Brough Castle
Previous page: Durham Cathedral

Contents

Short, easy walks

Walks of modest length, likely to involve some modest uphill walking

More challenging walks which may be longer and/or over more rugged terrain, often with some stiff climbs

Keymap 1

SCALE 1:263 157 or 1 INCH to about 4¼ MILES 1CM to 2.6KM

KILOMETRES

MILES

KEYMAP HEIGHTS SHOWN IN FEET

SCALE 1:263 157 or 1 INCH to about 4¼ MILES *1CM to 2.6KM*

KILOMETRES

MILES

KEYMAP HEIGHTS SHOWN IN FEET

CORSTOPITVM · Newton · Ovingham · Corbridge · A69
Haydon Bridge · HEXHAM · Low Gate · Dilston · Ovington · Cas
R South Tyne · 982 · B6305 · B6305

Catton · Dalton · Juniper · Staley · Healey · Hedley on the Hill · Chopwe
Allendale Town · Whitley Chapel · SLALEY FOREST · Minsteracres · DERE STREET · Hamsterl
1229 · Hexhamshire Common · Broadwell Ho · Blanchland Moor · Whittonstall · Newlands
1467 · 1345 · Carterway Heads · BB3 · CONSETT
Sinderhope · Allendale Common · 1400 · Blanchland · Edmundbyers · Derwent Resr · A68 · B6278 · Knitsley
1640 · 1259 · Muggleswick · Castleside
Green Hill · Nookton Fell · Hunstanworth · 1231 · Muggleswick Common · Healeyfield
1876 · Byerhope Resr · 1567 · Hisehope Resr · Smiddy Shaw Resr
Shield · Allenheads · Bolt's Law · Waskerley · 22
1840 · 1773 · Waskerley Resr
Stangend Currick · Middlehope Moor · Rookhope · Stanhope Common · 1694 · Collier Law · Tunstall Resr · Wolsingham Park Moor
Cornriggs · 1977 · Cowshill · Crawleyside · Stanhope · B6
Burnhope Resr · Wearhead · Westgate · Eastgate · 1 · Wolsingham · B6296 · Thor
Ireshopeburn · 7 · Weardale · Frosterley · 20
St John's Chapel · Daddry Shield · Hill End · White Kirkley · 2321
Ireshope Moor · Chapelfell Top · Snowhope Hill · Bollihope Common · St John's Hall
Three Pikes · 2284 · Westernhope Moor · 1599 · Pikeston Fell · Redford · Toll
23 · Langdon Common · 2216 · Newbiggin Common · Pawlaw Pike · Toll
18 · Langdon Beck · Middleton Common · 1854 · Bel
Widdybank Fell · Ettersgill · Newbiggin · HAMSTERLEY FOREST · 11
Cauldron Snout · Forest-in-Teesdale · Eggleston Common · Woodland · 1046
Cronkley Fell · High Force · 25 · Holwick · Woodland Fell · Copley
Mickle Fell · Middleton-in-Teesdale · 1511 · B6282 · Butt
2591 · LUNE FOREST · Lune Moor · 27 · Eggleston · Stainton
Bowbank · Mickleton · 15
Thringarth · Grassholme Resr · Romaldkirk
Grains o' th' Beck · River Lune · Grassholme · Hunderthwaite · Kinninvie
Dow Crag · Selset Resr · Hury · Cotherstone
1843 · Hunderthwaite Moor · Hury Resr · Lartington · B6277
Stainmore Common · Balderhead Resr · Blackton Resr · Deep Dale · ROMA
North Stainmore · Clove Lodge · 1025 · Pennine Way · Castle · 24
Cotherstone Moor · BARNARD CASTLE
South Stainmore · 1439 · Startforth · Boldron · Egglestone Abbey
Brough · 1689 · A67 · 17
Sowerby · A66 · 13 · ROMAN ROAD · Bowes · 28 · Brignall · ROAD
Kaber · 1701 · Castle · River Greta · Greta B
85 · Heggerscales · Moudy Mea · Scargill · Barningham
Winton · BOWES MOOR · STAINMORE FOREST · 726
BY · Winton Fell · 2171 · Sleightholme · 1463 · Scargill High Moor · Barningham Moor
HEN · Sleightholme Moor · Cleasby Hill · Hope · The Stang · 1466
Tan Hill · 1674 · 1816

UPON TYNE
Tyne Tunnel
Harton
Marsden Bay
15
RYTON
BLAYDON
HEBBURN
Whitbur
Walker
Pelaw
Monkton
Cleadon
277
A184
Greenside
Barlow
A1
Ouston
Felling
A194(M)
Boldon Colliery
A1018
Fulwell
WHICKHAM
GATESHEAD
Wrekenton
BOLDON
Roker
SUN
Highfield
A692
Sunniside
Lamesley
Kibblesworth
Castletown
South Hylton
A1231
Southwick
Hendon
ROWLANDS GILL
10
A6076
Birtley
WASHINGTON
3
A690
Ryhope
Burnopfield
Hobson
Tanfield
Ouston
Penshaw
B1286
New Silksworth
Doxford Park
STANLEY
A693
Beamish
Fatfield
A183
Herrington
Shiney Row
HOUGHTON-LE-SPRING
Seaton
A693
South Moor
Grange Villa
Pelton
Bournmoor
Fence Houses
A19
HETTON-LE-HOLE
Murton
Dalton-le-Dale
Annfield Plain
Craghead
Waldridge
CHESTER-LE-STREET
Great Lumley
East Rainton
West Rainton
Cold Hesled
Maiden Law
842
Edmondsley
A1(M)
Plawsworth
Easington Lane
South Hetton
Hawthorn
A19
Lanchester
Burnhope
Sacriston
Kibblesworth
Finchale Priory
Pittington
Littletown
A1(M)
B1283
Quebec
Esh
Witton Gilbert
Framwellgate Moor
A690
Haswell
Shotton Colliery
Langley Park
Bearpark
A691
9
Carrville
Sherburn
Ludworth
Thornley
Shotton
PETERL
Esh Winning
Waterhouses
New Brancepeth
DURHAM
Shadforth
B1279
Wheatley Hill
Castle Eden
4
BRANDON
840
Brancepeth
A1(M)
Bowburn
634
Quarrington Hill
Wingate
Trimdon Colliery
Station Town
CROOK
Billy Row
Oakenshaw
Sunderland Bridge
Coxhoe
Kelloe
Hutton Henry
A690
WILLINGTON
Croxdale
Hett
Tudhoe
A167
Trimdon Grange
Hunwick
Byers Green
SPENNYMOOR
Cornforth
Trimdon
Fishburn
Crookfoot Resr
High Grange
16
A688
Middlestone Moor
Kirk Merrington
Ferryhill
Chilton Lane
Bishop Middleham
Sedgefield
A689
Escomb
Coundon
Chilton
Bradbury
A177
Wynyard Village
Wolviston
BISHOP AUCKLAND
A689
Rushyford
Thorpe Larches
2
SHILDON
A167
Coundon Grange
Middridge
Mordon
Thorpe Thewles
West Auckland
A6072
NEWTON AYCLIFFE
A1(M)
Stillington
Whitton
Carlton
Norton
Wackerfield
Redworth
373
Elstob
STOCKTON-ON-TEES
Hilton
Bolam
Brafferton
Great Stainton
Bishopton
Redmarshall
Ingleton
Heighington
Little Stainton
Elton
Langton
Denton
Coatham Mundeville
A167
Sadberge
A66
Longnewton
Headlam
Walworth
Barmpton
Urlay Nook
Eaglescliffe
Gainford
Piercebridge
High Coniscliffe
Great Burdon
DARLINGTON
Egglescliffe
Low Coniscliffe
Cleasby
A66
Middleton St George
Yarm
A66(M)
Manfield
A66(M)
Hurworth-on-Tees
Teesside International Airport
Stanwick Camp
Stapleton
Low Dinsdale
Neasham
Low Worsall
Kirklevington
Stanwick St John
A1(M)
Croft-on-Tees
Picton
A66
Barton
Melsonby
Dalton-on-Tees
Eryholme
Girsby

Walk	Page	Start	Nat. Grid Reference	Distance Point	Time	Highest
Alston and the South Tyne Valley	64	Alston station	NY 716467	7½ miles (12.1km)	3½ hrs	1181ft (360m)
Appleby, Rutter Force and the River Eden	70	Appleby-in-Westmorland	NY 683203	8½ miles (13.7km)	4½ hrs	545ft (166m)
Around Dufton Pike	38	Dufton	NY 689250	5½ miles (8.9km)	3 hrs	1017ft (310m)
Auckland Park, Escomb and the River Wear	49	Bishop Auckland	NZ 211301	7½ miles (12.1km)	4 hrs	459ft (140m)
Barnard Castle, Cotherstone and the River Tees	73	Barnard Castle	NZ 050163	8½ miles (13.7km)	4½ hrs	623ft (190m)
Bowes Moor	86	Bowes	NY 995135	10½ miles (16.9km)	5½ hrs	1280ft (390m)
Brough Castle and Great Musgrave	28	Church Brough	NY 793140	5 miles (8km)	2½ hrs	623ft (190m)
Castle Eden Dene	20	Castle Eden Dene, Oakerside Lodge	NZ 427393	2½ miles (4km)	1½ hrs	295ft (90m)
Castle Eden Walkway and Thorpe Wood	16	Castle Eden Walkway Country Park	NZ 403244	3½ miles (5.6km)	2 hrs	213ft (65m)
Cauldron Snout	55	Langdon Beck	NY 847309	6½ miles (10.5km)	3½ hrs	1640ft (500m)
Causey Arch and Beamish Woods	33	Beamish Country Park	NZ 205561	5 miles (8km)	2½ hrs	558ft (170m)
Cox Green and Penshaw Hill	18	Cox Green	NZ 326552	3½ miles (5.6km)	1½ hrs	446ft (136m)
Crosthwaite Common, Rake Gill and Holwick	82	Middleton-in-Teesdale	NY 946254	9½ miles (15.3km)	4½ hrs	1673ft (510m)
Durham – Riverside and Woods	30	Durham, Market Place	NZ 274425	5 miles (8km)	2½ hrs	344ft (105m)
Egglestone Abbey, Paradise and the Meeting of the Waters	52	Egglestone Abbey, nr Barnard Castle	NZ 062150	7 miles (11.3km)	3 hrs	443ft (135m)
Hamsterley Forest	36	Hamsterley Forest Visitor Centre	NZ 092312	5 miles (8km)	2½ hrs	820ft (250m)
High and Low Force	77	Middleton-in-Teesdale	NY 906282	8½ miles (13.7km)	4½ hrs	1378ft (420m)
High Cup Nick	80	Dufton	NY 689250	8 miles (12.9km)	4 hrs	1870ft (570m)
Kirkby Stephen and Nateby	40	Kirkby Stephen	NY 775087	6½ miles (10.5km)	3½ hrs	787ft (240m)
Lazonby and Kirkoswald	43	Lazonby, Bridge End	NY 549403	6½ miles (10.5km)	3½ hrs	525ft (160m)
Marsden Rock and Whitburn	46	Marsden Bay	NZ 397651	7 miles (11.3km)	3½ hrs	262ft (80m)
Ravenstonedale	22	Ravenstonedale	NY 723042	4 miles (6.4km)	2 hrs	951ft (290m)
St John's Chapel and Westgate	26	St John's Chapel	NY 886378	4½ miles (7.2km)	2½ hrs	1312ft (400m)
Staindrop	24	Staindrop	NZ 127205	4½ miles (7.2km)	2½ hrs	476ft (145m)
Stanhope	14	Stanhope	NY 995393	2½ miles (4km)	1½ hrs	722ft (220m)
Talkin Tarn and Gelt Woods	58	Talkin Tarn Country Park	NY 544590	7 miles (11.3km)	3½ hrs	525ft (160m)
Waskerley Way	67	Waskerley	NZ 052453	7½ miles (12.1km)	4 hrs	1148ft (350m)
Wolsingham and the Weardale Way	61	Wolsingham	NZ 073366	7½ miles (12.1km)	3 hrs	1214ft (370m)

On the outward leg, the Pennine Way is followed through the austere terrain of the South Tyne valley; the return is alongside the track of the South Tynedale Railway.

This beautiful and varied walk in the Eden valley visits an impressive waterfall, passes through a remote village with an interesting church, and finishes with a lovely stroll beside the river.

After an initial walk through a gorge, the route encircles the base of the conically shaped Dufton Pike. There are magnificent views of the North Pennines and across the Eden valley to the Lakeland fells.

There is plenty of historic interest on this walk in the Wear valley. It includes the palace and former hunting-ground of the Bishops of Durham, a Victorian viaduct and a Saxon church.

An outstandingly attractive Teesdale walk, which keeps above the river for most of the way, apart from the final stretch where you descend to the wooded banks of the Tees.

There is a tremendous feeling of spaciousness and isolation on this route which, apart from an opening stretch beside the River Greta, is entirely across open and exposed moorland.

The Norman keep of Brough Castle is in sight for much of the way and there are impressive views of the North Pennines and a short stretch beside the River Eden.

The walk takes you along both sides of one of the steep-sided and thickly wooded denes that run down to the Durham coast.

Starting at a former railway station, the combination of a disused railway track and pleasant woodland makes for an attractive and interesting walk.

There are easier ways of reaching Cauldron Snout but this route provides real excitement as the path follows the River Tees through an ever-narrowing gorge to the foot of the waterfall.

The world's earliest railway bridge, which spans a wooded gorge, is the main focal point of this route. There is fine woodland walking, and the route passes by Beamish Open Air Museum.

The Doric temple on Penshaw Hill is the climax of this Weardale walk. It was built as a memorial to 'Radical' Jack Lambton, the Liberal politician who died in 1840, and is a magnificent viewpoint.

The middle part of this triangular walk follows a little-used bridleway over grouse moors so a compass may prove useful. Both of the other legs are straightforward, the return being on the banks of the Tees.

Much attractive riverside and woodland walking is enhanced by the dramatic views of Durham Cathedral and Castle, rising above the River Wear at both the start and finish.

This walk follows both banks of the River Tees past a famous beauty spot, the Meeting of the Waters, where the River Greta joins the Tees. It provided the subject for one of Turner's finest landscapes.

The walk uses waymarked trails to create a most attractive and easy-to-follow route through part of County Durham's largest forest.

High Force has a drop of 70ft (21m) and is the mightiest of English waterfalls. This walk takes you to its best viewpoint and then follows the Tees upstream. The return is on lanes and field paths.

From Dufton a steady climb along the Pennine Way leads to a dramatic chasm. On the return you enjoy the most superb views across the Eden valley to the Lakeland fells.

There is a series of impressive views of both the North Pennines and the Howgills on this Eden valley walk. The opening stretch is by the river.

There are two attractive sandstone villages, extensive views across the Eden valley and an attractive final stretch beside the river on this walk.

The walk first heads inland over the gentle slopes of the Cleadon Hills and finishes with an exhilarating walk along the coast, passing by a series of rocky and sandy bays.

This is a flat and easy walk that gives fine views of the Howgill Fells and passes by a nature reserve. Be prepared for plenty of stiles.

This walk in Upper Weardale passes by remains of former lead mines and finishes with a pleasant stroll by the river.

Starting from one of Durham's prettiest villages, the walk takes you across fields, by streams and alongside woodland.

Fine views up and down the River Wear can be enjoyed on this short walk around Stanhope.

The tranquil beauty of Talkin Tarn is enjoyed at the start and finish; in between there is a dramatic walk through a thickly wooded gorge.

Unlike many of the longer walks in this book, this one can be attempted when conditions are less than perfect. It uses a long section of disused railway as well as field and woodland paths.

This is a long walk with no severe gradients. It provides an opportunity to enjoy the scenery of Weardale, which can be just as attractive as that of Teesdale to the south.

At-a-glance...

Introduction to Durham, North Pennines and Tyne & Wear

For centuries the main route across the North Pennines has been through the Stainmore Gap, now occupied by the busy A66, and at its highest point is the county boundary between Cumbria and Durham. At both ends of the gap – Brough in the west and Bowes in the east – are the remains of Norman castles situated within the earthworks of earlier Roman forts, a clear indication of the strategic importance of this route.

This walking guide covers both the Cumbrian and Durham sides of the North Pennines, a designated Area of Outstanding Natural Beauty, and also extends eastwards across Durham to the North Sea coast. It embraces the traditional – pre-1974 – boundaries of County Durham, i.e. all the land between the Tees and the Tyne, and therefore includes the areas of the metropolitan county of Tyne & Wear to the south of the Tyne, as well as parts of former Cleveland to the north of the Tees.

Castles and churches

For much of its history this has been a frontier zone. Just to the north is Hadrian's Wall and there are several remains of Roman forts in the area. Medieval castles are in abundance: some of the finest are at Brough, Brougham and Appleby in Cumbria, and Barnard Castle, Bowes and Raby in County Durham, plus, of course, the great episcopal castle at Durham itself. After the union of the crowns in 1603 largely ended centuries of war with Scotland, these castles either became picturesque ruins or were converted into more comfortable residences. Durham Castle was given a different role; in 1836 the bishop gave it to the new University of Durham as its foundation college.

In the Anglo-Saxon period, the region was the heartland of early Northumbrian Christianity and today contains some of the finest surviving Saxon churches in England. Two in particular are the tiny church at Escomb in the Wear valley and the church and monastic site at Jarrow, where the Venerable Bede, 'Father of English History', lived and worked. This is now part of the fascinating and imaginative Bede's World complex.

Focal point of the region is the city of Durham, one of Britain's finest and most attractive historic cities. The cathedral – described by Sir Walter Scott as 'half church of God, half castle 'gainst the Scot' – and castle stand side by side on a wooded cliff above a horseshoe bend in the River Wear. They make an unforgettable sight and have deservedly been given World Heritage status. It was in 995, after many years of wandering from place to place, that the remains of St Cuthbert found a permanent home here and the diocese was established. In the late 11th century the Normans erected the mighty cathedral, one of the finest in Europe, and built the castle, twin symbols of the enormous power exercised by the medieval bishops of Durham. They were prince bishops – a phrase much used by

View of the Howgill Fells near Ravenstonedale

the local tourist authorities to promote the area – granted virtually sovereign powers by Norman kings in return for protecting this vulnerable border area from Scottish invasions. The bishops raised their own armies and taxes, minted their own coinage and had their own courts.

Industry and towns

Industry has always been a major factor in this area. From the 16th century onwards, lead-mining flourished in the remote valleys and hills of the North Pennines, reaching its height in the Victorian era. This has now gone, but the remains of some of the mines can still be seen, especially in Upper Weardale, and there are lead-mining museums at Killhope and Nenthead.

Biggest impact of all on the landscape of the region was the development of the Durham coalfield and the growth of shipbuilding on the Tyne and Wear, both reaching their zenith during the Industrial Revolution. This was one of Britain's most prolific coal-producing areas, and the mines even extended to the coast and under the sea. Transporting the coal to the nearest rivers – Tyne, Wear and Tees – was a major problem and this was overcome by the creation of wooden waggonways, the forerunners of the railways, pioneered in this part of the country. Causey Arch, near Stanley, claims to be the world's earliest-surviving railway bridge, and George Stephenson's Stockton to Darlington Railway, opened in 1825, was the first railway in the world to use steam-powered locomotives.

During the Industrial Revolution the medieval city of Durham was soon outgrown by the rise of the industrial towns of Gateshead, Stockton and Darlington and the great ports of South Shields, Sunderland and Hartlepool, the latter group mostly engaged in coal exporting and shipbuilding. Now the coal mines and shipyards have gone and the Industrial Revolution has largely receded into history, but an excellent way of appreciating the industrial heritage of the area is to spend a day at the Open Air Museum at Beamish, not far from the Causey Arch, a living and working experience of life in the North of England at the beginning of the 20th century.

Geography

Tourist literature describes the North Pennines as 'England's last wilderness' and there is some justification in that claim. It is an excellent walking area and one that tends to get neglected in favour of the nearby Lake District, Yorkshire Dales and Northumberland national parks. Its huge expanses of wild and open moorland include some of the highest peaks in the Pennine range, and on both sides sparkling rivers wind their way through lovely dales and across lush lowland pastures to the sea. There are also remote and unspoilt villages and fine market towns: Barnard Castle, Kirkby Stephen, Appleby and Alston. The latter is the highest in England and is often cut off during a hard winter.

On the western slopes is the lovely valley of the Eden, and the river eventually flows through Carlisle and on into the Solway Firth. From the higher points, magnificent views extend over the Eden valley to the outline of the Lakeland mountains and on across the Solway to the Galloway hills on the horizon. To the south, the smooth grassy slopes of the Howgill Fells fill the skyline, forming a 'bridge' between the Pennines and the Cumbrian mountains.

For first time visitors to the area, perhaps expecting nothing but coal mines and industrial towns, County Durham may well come as something of a pleasant surprise. Extending eastwards from the slopes of the Pennines are Teesdale and Weardale, as beautiful as any of the better-known dales of Yorkshire and Derbyshire and well-wooded in their lower reaches.

Remains of Brough Castle

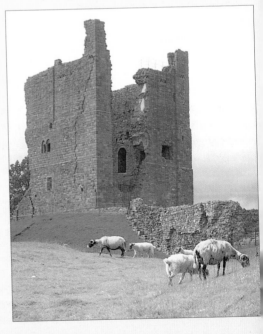

Between Teesdale and Weardale are the wooded expanses of Hamsterley Forest, a fine recreational area with superb walking facilities. The Wear valley and the area to the north was the heart of the Durham coalfield but the mines have closed and most of the area has been land-scaped and made green again.

East Durham is noted for its denes, thickly wooded and steep-sided valleys, which stretch like fingers to the North Sea coast. The coast itself, despite being

Dufton Pike, from the walk to High Cup Nick

heavily urbanised and industrialised, is not without its attractions. There are fine sandy beaches and a particularly dramatic stretch in Tyne & Wear between South Shields and Sunderland, with a series of stacks and rock arches, including the famous Marsden Rock.

Walking in the area

The Pennine Way weaves its way across the North Pennines, both making use of the river valleys and taking a high-level moorland route in places. There are other waymarked long-distance paths – Teesdale Way and Weardale Way – and in County Durham there is a network of former railway tracks that have been converted into footpaths and cycleways, many of them originally built to link the coal mines with the main rail network.

Visitors to the area will find walks to suit all tastes and all levels of fitness. The North Pennines may well be 'England's last wilderness' but both here and in County Durham there is much more than wild moorland. Walkers can enjoy the challenge of some of the finest moorland terrain in the country if they wish, but for the less ambitious, or if the weather is unsuitable – always a crucial factor to take into consideration – there are plenty of more relaxing, low-level walks beside the rivers Tees, Wear and Eden, through woodlands and forests, by the coast and along some of the former railway tracks.

Stanhope

Start	Stanhope
Distance	2½ miles (4km)
Approximate time	1½ hours
Parking	Durham Dales Centre, Stanhope
Refreshments	Pubs and cafés at Stanhope, tearoom at Durham Dales Centre
Ordnance Survey maps	Landranger 92 (Barnard Castle & surrounding area), Outdoor Leisure 31 (North Pennines – Teesdale & Weardale)

This short and easy walk in Weardale is mainly along riverside paths and across meadows on both banks of the Wear. There are attractive views up and downstream and across the river to Stanhope from the south bank. The walk necessitates crossing stepping-stones at one point but if the river is high or the stones are likely to be slippery, there is an easier alternative crossing via a footbridge.

The former quarrying and lead-mining village of Stanhope stands on the north bank of the River Wear. In the church-yard of the fine 12th-century church is the stump of a fossilised tree, placed here in 1962 and thought to be around 250 million years old. On the opposite side of the Market Place is Stanhope Castle, a large house built in the late 18th century. The walk starts at the Durham Dales Centre, which comprises a tourist information centre, shop, craft workshops and tearoom.

Begin by walking down to the road and turn left into the Market Place. Bear right along the Butts, by the Packhorse Inn, follow the road around a right bend and, before reaching the river, turn left Ⓐ – still along the Butts – to join the bank of the Wear.

Go through a metal kissing-gate to cross a railway line, go through another gate, bear left across a field and go through a kissing-gate on the far side.

Keep along the right edge of the next field, go through a kissing-gate in the corner, continue in the same direction across the corner of a sports field to rejoin the riverbank and bear left along it. Go through a kissing-gate in the field corner, recross the railway line, turn right through another kissing-gate and walk along a fence-lined path to yet another kissing-gate. After going through that, continue along the right edge of a field and climb a stone stile onto a lane Ⓑ.

Turn right to cross first a bridge over the river and then a railway bridge and, where the lane turns left, turn right, at public footpath and Weardale Way signs, along a tarmac track through a caravan site. At the far end of the site, keep ahead to climb a stile and continue along a tree-lined path above the river. The path descends to emerge from the trees and bends right to a stile. Climb it, walk along the left field edge and turn

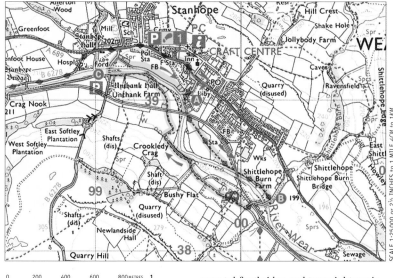

SCALE 1:25 000 or 2½ INCHES to 1 MILE 4CM to 1KM

```
0    200   400   600   800 METRES  1
                                   KILOMETRES
                                   MILES
0    200   400   600 YARDS    ½
```

left at a wall corner to continue, by a wire fence on the left, to the field corner. Climb a concrete ladder-stile to cross the railway line once more, climb a similar stile on the other side and walk along the left edge of a field, curving slightly left. On the far side, climb a stone stile and continue along a riverside track.

If you do not wish to use the stepping-stones to cross the Wear, turn right over a metal footbridge and turn right again on the other side to rejoin the full walk.

Otherwise continue along the track to a road **C** and turn right over the stepping-stones. There are a lot of them as the river is fairly wide at this point. Keep ahead along the road and, at the corner of a playing-field, turn right onto a tarmac path. This soon becomes a riverside promenade that continues between the river on the right and the boundary wall of Castle Park on the left. On reaching a road, turn left and retrace your steps to the start. ●

The River Wear at Stanhope

Castle Eden Walkway and Thorpe Wood

Castle Eden Walkway and Thorpe Wood

Start	Castle Eden Walkway Country Park, signposted from A177 between Sedgefield and Stockton-on-Tees
Distance	3½ miles (5.6km)
Approximate time	2 hours
Parking	Castle Eden Walkway Country Park
Refreshments	Snacks and soft drinks at Visitor Centre
Ordnance Survey maps	Landranger 93 (Middlesbrough, Darlington & Hartlepool), Pathfinders 591, NZ 42/52 (Billingham & Tees Mouth) and 590, NZ 22/32 (Newton Aycliffe)

The walk begins with a pleasant and easy stroll along the track of a disused railway. It continues across fields and ends with a ramble through the beautiful Thorpe Wood, a nature reserve. In such tranquil surroundings, it is difficult to believe that industrial Teesside is so close, but on the more open middle section of the route the views extend right across Teesside to the line of the Cleveland Hills.

On Castle Eden Walkway

From the car park go through a kissing-gate, signposted 'Visitor Centre and Toilets', turn right and then left and climb steps to the Station House Visitor Centre, housed in the former Thorpe Thewles station buildings. Castle Eden Walkway and Country Park is based around a stretch of the former Castle Eden Branch Railway, opened in the 1870s to carry coal from the Durham coalfield to the Tees estuary, and also includes Thorpe Wood.

Turn right along the former platform and continue along the tree-lined and well-surfaced track as far as the third bridge **A**. After passing under it, turn left up steps and left again at the top onto a track. Turn right along the track for a brief detour to the 12th-century ruins of Grindon church **B**, glimpsed in a field on the right but unfortunately not accessible.

Retrace your steps to the bridge **A**, cross it and, where the track bends left, keep ahead over a stile at a sign 'Grindon Footpath Loop to Thorpe

Wood'. Walk along the right edge of a field and, after bearing slightly right to climb a stile, continue through a belt of trees, emerging from them via another stile. Turn left and follow a broad, undulating, grassy track across fields, bearing slightly right by a line of trees and continuing to a T-junction. Turn right onto a descending track and, at the bottom, turn right through a kissing-gate to enter Thorpe Wood Nature Reserve **C**.

Follow a track through this lovely woodland and just after passing Thorpe Pond – constructed in the 1970s to attract wildfowl – turn left at a way-marked post **D**. The path crosses a burn, bends right and ascends a long flight of steps, curving left and continuing up to a kissing-gate. Go through, turn left and descend steps to rejoin the disused railway track. Turn left and retrace your steps to the start.   ●

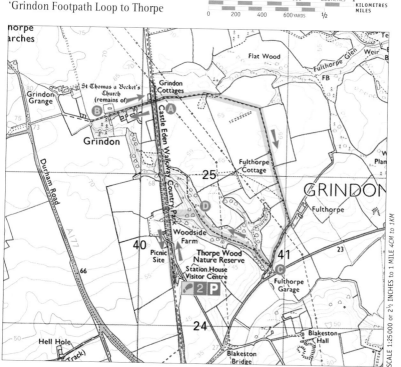

Cox Green and Penshaw Hill

Start	Cox Green, 3 miles (4.8km) west of Sunderland
Distance	3½ miles (5.6km)
Approximate time	1½ hours
Parking	Cox Green
Refreshments	Pubs at Cox Green and close to point **C** at Penshaw
Ordnance Survey maps	Landranger 88 (Tyneside & Durham), Pathfinder 562, NZ 25/35 (Washington & Chester-le-Street)

Many people must wonder about the monument on top of Penshaw Hill as they dash past it on the A19. It is a magnificent viewpoint – you can even see the distinctive shapes of the Cheviots from here on a good day – and it is also celebrated as being the place where the Lambton Worm lurked. The grooves on the hill – which are difficult to discern – are supposed to have been made when it coiled itself around it. Other parts of the walk use the River Wear Trail, a fine network of paths.

Cox Green is a delightful Wearside beauty spot with a large car park opposite the Oddfellows Arms pub. Until the latter part of the 19th century it was a busy port handling timber, coal and sandstone. Ships were built and repaired, the last being launched into the waters of the Wear in 1862 (there is still a boatyard for pleasure craft). Turn left at the river and follow the road past the handful of houses. Beyond these there is a narrow riverside path leading towards the Victoria Viaduct, which was opened in 1838 and takes the east coast main line across the valley. On the left there used to be tunnels that brought sandstone down to the riverside loading-staithes from the quarries at Low Lambton. Turn left off the riverside path at the notice-board before the viaduct. This is James Steel Park, named after the former Lord Lieutenant of

Durham, Sir James Steel, who was also the first chairman of the Washington Development Corporation. It extends for 2½ miles (4km) on both sides of the river.

Pass under the railway by the tunnel and then bear left to pass round the south and east sides of Low Lambton Farm (it feels like their front garden). Go under the railway again by the arch on the right **A** and on the other side turn left along the field edge. On meeting the hedgerow of the next field, turn right towards the monument and follow a much clearer path to the left of the hedge towards another railway embankment. Climb this to cross the old trackbed and then go down the other side to cross the road too. The well-used path runs up the right side of the field below electricity lines. At the top **B** turn left onto the road and then left

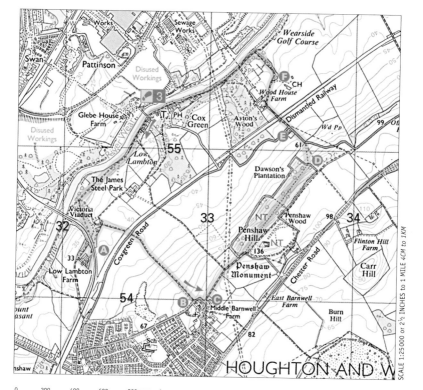

SCALE 1:25000 or 2½ INCHES to 1 MILE 4CM to 1KM

```
0     200    400    600    800 METRES   1
                                         KILOMETRES
                                         MILES
0     200    400    600 YARDS    ½
```

again **C** onto a path before new bun-
galows (if you need refreshment follow
the road for a few more steps to reach a
couple of pubs).

There are magnificent views from the
path and even better ones from the
monument itself. The Nissan factory is a
prominent landmark. Unexpectedly, the
monument is roofless, uncompleted. It
was built in the form of a Doric temple,
perhaps a copy of the Temple of Theseus
in Athens, to the memory of 'Radical'
Jack Lambton, the Liberal politician
who died in 1840.

The story of the Lambton Worm is
one of the most famous of north-
country legends. John, the heir to the
Lambton estates in medieval times, is
said to have slain the monstrous worm
but invoked a curse under which nine
lords of Lambton died unexpected

deaths. The terraces on the hill, said to
have been caused by the worm coiling
itself around it, are best seen on the
hill's south side. (Worm Hill close to the
Victoria Viaduct at Fatfield on the north
side of the Wear is also claimed to be a
resting-place of the serpent.)

From the monument, return to the
path below, which runs through the
woods on the lower slopes of the hill.
After the stile that leads the path out of
the woods **D**, cross the meadow diagonally to its lower left corner. Carry
straight on along the road, passing a
'Private Road' sign when the Cox Green
road goes off to the left, opposite an old
school **E**.

Follow this lane round towards the
golf club but leave it to take a path on
the left when the drive bears to the
right **F**. This descends to the river
through a peaceful, wooded little valley.
Turn left at the riverbank to complete
the walk.   ●

Castle Eden Dene

Start	Castle Eden Dene, Oakerside Lodge, just off Durham Way on the south side of Peterlee and signposted from town
Distance	2½ miles (4km)
Approximate time	1½ hours
Parking	Oakerside Lodge
Refreshments	None
Ordnance Survey maps	Landranger 93 (Middlesbrough, Darlington & Hartlepool), Pathfinder 573, NZ 43/44 & part of NZ 53 (Hartlepool & Peterlee)

Although some distance apart, the connection between this walk and Walk 2 is the former Castle Eden Branch Railway. Despite being a short walk, there are several quite steep ascents and descents on this highly attractive route through the steep-sided and thickly wooded dene, virtually a gorge, crossing the burn that runs through it several times.

Castle Eden Dene, now a National Nature Reserve, is one of a number of well-wooded ravines that stretch through the countryside of east Durham down to the North Sea coast. Its natural appearance is something of a deception because in the 18th century the dene was landscaped by the Burdon family, local landowners, in the 'Picturesque' style that was fashionable at the time, attempting to re-create on the Durham coast the idealised landscape of Italy. Many of the present paths and bridges over the burn were constructed at this time.

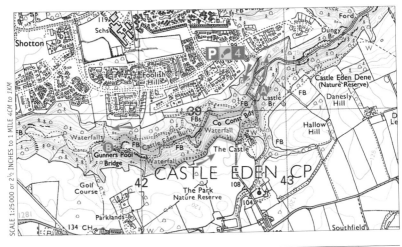

Castle Eden Dene

From the car park, go down steps, cross a track and go through a kissing-gate, by a National Nature Reserve notice-board. Take the track ahead, which curves right and descends into the wooded dene and, at a fork, continue along the left-hand track down to Castle Bridge **Ⓐ**. Do not cross it but turn right onto an undulating path above Castle Eden Burn, curving left to cross a footbridge over it below almost vertical cliffs.

Continue – now with the burn on the right – and the path climbs, via steps in places, passing more sheer cliffs. Ignoring a path coming in from the left, descend to the burn again, turn right to recross it and follow the path to the left, climbing steeply and bearing slightly left on meeting another path. At a fork, take the left-hand, lower path which descends and, when you see a footbridge (Gunner's Pool Bridge), turn left and head down to cross it **Ⓑ**. This is a beautiful spot, with the burn far below cascading over rocks at the bottom of the gorge.

After crossing the bridge, turn left and continue along the edge of the dene, crossing another footbridge. At the next fork, take the right-hand, upper path, which climbs to the top edge of the dene and then descends to a T-junction in front of an embankment. Turn left along a most attractive track that keeps by the right-hand, inside edge of the trees and, in front of a metal gate, turn left onto a track that heads downhill, curving first to the right and then taking the left-hand, lower track at a fork.

The track curves left and continues down to Castle Bridge. Cross it and, at the fork immediately ahead, **Ⓐ** take the left-hand track, here rejoining the outward route, and retrace your steps uphill to the start. ●

Ravenstonedale

Start	Ravenstonedale, parking-area at corner of road by school and church
Distance	4 miles (6.4km)
Approximate time	2 hours
Parking	By school and church at Ravenstonedale
Refreshments	Pubs at Ravenstonedale, pub at Crossbank
Ordnance Survey maps	Landranger 91 (Appleby-in-Westmorland), Outdoor Leisure 19 (Howgill Fells & Upper Eden Valley)

There are impressive views of the nearby Howgills on this pleasant and easy-paced walk through the valleys of Lockholme Beck and Scandal Beck. At the approximate half-way point there is the opportunity to explore a small nature reserve. Although a short and mostly flat walk, there are a large number of gated, stone stiles to negotiate, some of which are quite narrow. The route is well-waymarked throughout.

In the churchyard at Ravenstonedale are the slight remains of a small Gilbertine monastery founded around 1131. The church dates from the middle of the 18th century but incorporates parts of a medieval predecessor.

Begin by taking the road signposted to Sedbergh, turn right by the Black Swan and walk up the village street. Opposite the United Reformed church, turn left up steps, at a public footpath sign to Lockholme Head Ⓐ, and turn left along a path through bushes that bends right to a metal kissing-gate. Go through, walk along the left field edge, climb a gated, stone stile and keep ahead in a straight line – over a series of similar stiles and across a succession of fields – finally bearing right across a field corner to climb a stile onto a lane.

Cross over, climb the stone stile opposite and head diagonally across a field. Climb a stile, continue along the right edge of two fields – over two more

stone stiles – and after the second stile, turn right along a track. Cross Lockholme Beck and about 50 yds (46m) beyond, turn left over a stone stile Ⓑ.

Bear slightly right across a field, later heading gently downhill and continuing towards the farm buildings ahead. Climb a stone stile to the left of the farm, cross a track, climb the stone stile opposite and walk across a field to another stone stile. After climbing it, walk along the right field edge to join a track that passes to the left of the farmhouse and continues to a stile. Climb it, walk along the left edge of the next field, go through a gate and continue across a field, heading downhill and bearing slightly right to a stone stile in the corner.

Do not climb the stile but turn left Ⓒ along the field edge, by a wall on the right, go through a metal gate in the corner and cross a footbridge over the

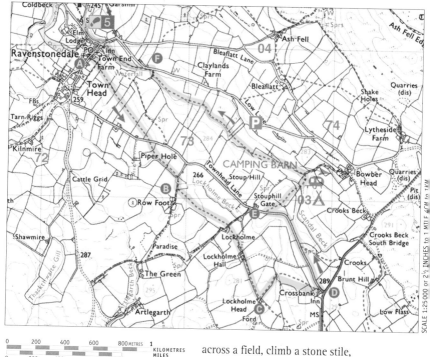

0 200 400 600 800 METRES 1
KILOMETRES
MILES
0 200 400 600 YARDS ½

beck. Turn right onto a permissive path that keeps along the right edge of the field, following it as it curves left. A gate on the right gives access to Crossbank Nature Reserve, a private reserve owned and created by the proprietor of the Fat Lamb Hotel. It is now managed under a Countryside Stewardship agreement and is open to all. No charge is made but visitors are welcome to partake of the food and drink available at the hotel.

Go through a kissing-gate, bear left uphill along the left field edge and bear right across the field corner to go through a gate. Behind is a particularly fine view over the nature reserve, with the Howgills prominent on the skyline. Keep ahead along a stony path that turns right, go through another gate and continue onto a lane by the Fat Lamb Inn **D**. Turn left along the lane and turn right through a metal gate, at a public footpath sign to Bowber Head or Ravenstonedale **E**. Head diagonally across a field, climb a stone stile, continue downhill along the right field edge and go through a gate.

Cross a footbridge over Scandal Beck, turn left across rough grass to cross another footbridge over a narrower beck and continue across to climb a stone stile. Walk along the left edge of a field, turn left to cross another foot-bridge over a beck, climb a stone stile and turn right to head diagonally across a field, making for a stone stile in the far left corner. Climb it and continue along the left edge of a succession of fields and over a series of gated, stone stiles, with Scandal Beck on the left. In the corner of the last field, turn right to go through a gate, cross a footbridge over a beck and keep ahead to a lane **F**.

Turn left and, where the lane bears right, keep ahead over a stone stile, at a public footpath sign to Ravenstonedale. Continue alongside the beck and climb two more stone stiles until you reach a lane. Turn left and turn right by the Black Swan to retrace your steps to the start.

Staindrop

Start	Staindrop
Distance	4½ miles (7.2km)
Approximate time	2½ hours
Parking	Roadside parking beside one of the greens at Staindrop
Refreshments	Pubs and cafés at Staindrop
Ordnance Survey maps	Landranger 92 (Barnard Castle & surrounding area), Pathfinders 580, NZ 12/13 (Crook & West Auckland) and 599, NZ 01/11 (Barnard Castle & Gainford)

Much of the first part of this well-waymarked and mainly flat walk is by the banks of the delightful Sudburn Beck. The route then continues across fields and along the edge of woodland to return to Staindrop, a most attractive village. From many points there are fine views across the surrounding countryside.

Staindrop is an outstanding example of a 'green village' – a characteristic of County Durham – with long, wide greens enclosed by mostly 17th- and 18th-century buildings. At the east end of the village is the impressive medieval church, the 'Cathedral of the Dales', which dates back to the Norman period but was extended and rebuilt in succeeding centuries. Inside are the tombs of some of the powerful Neville family, who lived at nearby Raby Castle, a clue as to why such a large and imposing church should be found in this relatively small village.

The walk begins by the post office. Cross the road, pass to the right of the buildings opposite (Central Buildings), walk across the green and continue along the narrow Stangarth Lane to the right of the Scarth Memorial Hall. Where the lane ends, turn right Ⓐ along a track to a stile, climb it and bear left across a field to climb another stile and cross a bridge over a beck. Continue across the field to climb a stile on the

far side, keep in the same direction across the next field and climb a stone stile onto a road just to the right of a bridge Ⓑ.

Cross the road, climb a stone stile, walk across a field to climb another one and continue along a path beside the tree-lined bank of Sudburn Beck. Keep by the beck, along the edge of meadows and over a succession of stiles, finally climbing steps onto a road to the right of Sudburn Bridge. Cross over, pass beside a gate, climb the stone stile in front and bear slightly left across a field to a stile. Climb it and continue in the same direction across the next field to rejoin the beck. After climbing a stile, look out in the next field for where you turn left over another stile to continue beside the beck. Climb a stile, keep ahead to go through a gate and just beyond that is a footbridge over the beck Ⓒ.

Do not turn left over it but turn right, head up a slope and, at the top, bear right to go through a gate by a wall corner. Immediately turn left over a

Staindrop village green

tarmac drive to a road.

Turn right and at a public footpath sign after about 200 yds (183m), turn left **E** along the drive to West Lodge. In front of the lodge, turn right through a gate and – apart from a slight deviation to pass to the right of the garden of another lodge – continue along the left edge of a series of fields and over a succession of stiles, keeping beside a wall bordering Raby Wood. Just before reaching the end of the last field, follow the path as it bends right across to a stone stile in the far corner. Climb it, walk along the right edge of two fields and about half-way across the second one, look out for a gap in the hedge on the right and go through it.

stile, keep ahead across a field, passing to the right of a large house (Snotterton Hall), and climb a stile to continue along a track. From this track there are extensive views over rolling and well-wooded country, with the tower of Staindrop church clearly visible. Just before the track bends right, turn left **D** through a gate and walk along the left field edge to a gate in the corner. Go through that, veer slightly right across the next field and on the far side, look out for where you turn right through a gate. Head gently downhill in the direction of Scaife House, pass between gateposts and cross a beck at the bottom. Continue uphill across the next field, walk through the farmyard and along a

Turn left along a narrow path, between a hedge on the left and a wire fence on the right, go through a squeezer stile and continue along a walled path to emerge onto North Green in Staindrop. Keep ahead to the start. ●

0	200	400	600	800 METRES	1
					KILOMETRES
					MILES
0	200	400	600 YARDS	½	

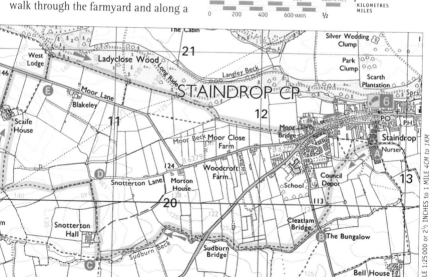

St John's Chapel and Westgate

St John's Chapel and Westgate

Start	St John's Chapel
Distance	4½ miles (7.2km)
Approximate time	2½ hours
Parking	St John's Chapel
Refreshments	Pubs at St John's Chapel, pub at Westgate
Ordnance Survey maps	Landrangers 91 (Appleby-in-Westmorland) or 92 (Barnard Castle & surrounding area), Outdoor Leisure 31 (North Pennines – Teesdale & Weardale)

From the village of St John's Chapel, the route heads uphill and continues along the north side of Weardale, passing by abandoned quarries and former lead mines before descending into Westgate. Most of the remainder of the walk is along or close to the banks of the River Wear. There are fine views over Upper Weardale and some pleasant riverside walking.

Now a quiet backwater, St John's Chapel was once a busy town and important centre of lead-mining and quarrying in Upper Weardale. The Georgian church, on the site of the original medieval chapel, and Victorian town hall are evidence of its former heyday. From the car park, turn left along the road into the Market Place,

The River Wear near St John's Chapel

where you turn right along a lane that passes between the church on the right and town hall on the left. Where the lane bends right, turn left **Ⓐ** along a narrower lane, cross a bridge over a burn and immediately turn right, at a public footpath sign, to a kissing-gate.

Go through, take the tarmac path across a field and cross a footbridge over the River Wear. Keep ahead to continue alongside a wall, climb steps, go through a kissing-gate, continue up more steps and, at the top, keep straight ahead across a field and climb a stone stile onto a lane. Cross over, climb the stone stile opposite and continue uphill across a field, bearing right away from the boundary wall, to a stone stile. Climb that

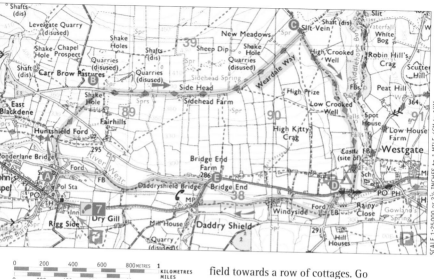

and continue ascending, climbing two more stone stiles to emerge onto a lane **B**.

Turn right and keep along the lane to where it ends, a distance of about 1 mile (1.6km). All the way there are fine views to the right across Upper Weardale, and you pass the remains of some of the abandoned quarries and former lead mines for which this area was famous in the 19th century. On reaching the end of the lane, turn right **C** through a metal gate and follow a track downhill, going through a series of metal gates and finally continuing down a path to a gate in the bottom corner of a field. Go through, keep ahead along a track between farm buildings and continue down to a road in Westgate.

The pub and main part of the village is to the left; the route continues to the right. Take the first lane on the left **D** – just beyond a garage – cross a footbridge over the River Wear (by a ford) and at a public footpath sign, turn right along a track, passing in front of cottages, to a kissing-gate. Go through, walk across a meadow to go through another kissing-gate, keep ahead by a fence on the left and continue across a

field towards a row of cottages. Go through a metal gate and walk along a tarmac track in front of the cottages. Just before the end of this track, turn right across grass, turn left to cross a footbridge over a burn and then climb a ladder-stile and cross a plank footbridge over another small burn in quick succession.

Keep ahead beside the river but, on reaching the first trees on the left, bear left off the riverside path and head up an embankment to a gate at the corner of a fence and wall. Go through the gate, walk along the right field edge, above sloping woodland, and turn right over a stone stile in the corner. Turn left to continue along the top of the embankment – now with a wall on the left – climb a stile, keep ahead and climb three more stiles to emerge onto a road at Daddry Shield. Turn right and, just before Daddryshield Bridge, turn left at a public footpath sign **E** to descend steps to the river. Cross a footbridge over a tributary burn, go through a gate and along a riverside path.

Keep beside the Wear, going through a succession of kissing-gates, and the path eventually emerges onto a narrow lane, by a footbridge, ford and stepping-stones. Turn left and follow the lane to the start. ●

Brough Castle
and Great Musgrave

Start	Church Brough
Distance	5 miles (8km)
Approximate time	2½ hours
Parking	Church Brough
Refreshments	None *en route* but pubs and cafés at nearby Market Brough
Ordnance Survey maps	Landranger 91 (Appleby-in-Westmorland), Outdoor Leisure 19 (Howgill Fells & Upper Eden Valley)

For much of the way, the imposing Norman keep of Brough Castle is in sight as you proceed through the valley of Swindale Beck to near where it flows into the River Eden by St Theobald's church. The return leg leads through the quiet village of Great Musgrave and across fields back to Church Brough.

Both Roman and Norman conquerors realised the strategic importance of the site occupied by Brough Castle, built by the Normans within the earthworks of an earlier Roman fort. The site guards the western end of the Stainmore road, one of the most important routes across the Pennines, as evidenced by its present use by the busy A66. Near the castle is the medieval church, dating from the 12th century but with later additions. By the later Middle Ages, the original settlement of Church Brough had been overtaken by Market Brough as the main village and the latter became an important stopping-place during the heyday of the stage coaches in the 18th and early 19th centuries.

Begin by turning down the lane towards the church, which degenerates into a rough track. At a fork, take the right-hand track, climb a stile and head uphill to reach a gate. To the right are grand views of Brough Castle, backed by the line of the North Pennines. Go through the gate, head downhill along the left edge of a field, turn right beside a barn and continue along a left field edge to another gate.

After going through the gate, continue gently downhill across a field – keeping to the left of a pair of trees – go through a gate, bear slightly right by the corner of some trees and head across the field to go through another gate on the far side. Continue by the left edge of a meadow bordering Swindale Beck and on the far side go through a gate onto a track **A**. Turn right to cross a footbridge over the beck, turn left at a T-junction in front of a farm and go through a gate, at a public footpath sign to Lane Head.

Keep ahead uphill across a field – briefly joining a wire fence bordering trees on the left – and after this fence bears left, keep straight ahead to pass through a gap in a hedgeline and continue towards a farm, making for a stone stile. Climb it, go through a gate by a wall corner and keep alongside farm

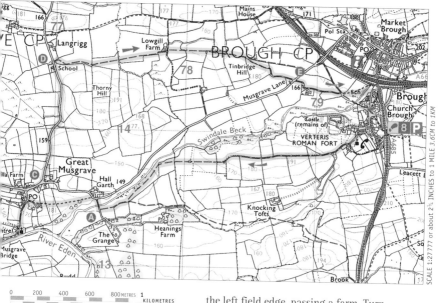

SCALE 1:27777 or about 2¼ INCHES to 1 MILE 3.6CM to 1KM

| 0 | 200 | 400 | 600 | 800 METRES | 1 |
| 0 | 200 | 400 | 600 YARDS | ½ | KILOMETRES MILES |

buildings on the left. Follow a tarmac drive to the right, go through gates, keep ahead to a T-junction and turn left along another tarmac drive at a public footpath sign to St Theobald's Church.

In front of gates, bear slightly left along an enclosed tarmac path that descends to the church, which stands in a shady and secluded position on the banks of the River Eden. The present building dates from 1845 and is the third on the site. Climb a stile in front of the church, turn right along the river-bank to Musgrave Bridge, go through a gate beside it and turn right along a lane **B**. At a T-junction, turn right into the village of Great Musgrave and, at a fork in front of a telephone-box, take the left-hand, lower lane **C**. Keep along it for just over ½ mile (800m) and, at a public footpath sign to Brough, turn right through a gate **D**.

Walk along the right field edge to go through a gate and head diagonally across the next field to a gate on the far side. Brough Castle comes into view again. Go through the gate, keep ahead to go through another and continue by the left field edge, passing a farm. Turn left through a gate in front of the farm, immediately turn right through another gate and walk across a field to a gate in the far left corner. Go through, keep in the same direction across the next field and go through a gate to the left of a barn. Keep along the left edge of a field, go through a gate at the far end and continue along the right edge of a field, above an embankment on the left, to reach two gates.

Go through the right-hand gate, walk along the right field edge and, in the corner, turn right along an enclosed track. Go through a gate, and the track curves left through another gate to a lane **E**. Take the track opposite – public footpath sign Church Brough – which curves first right and then left and in front of gates, bear left along a hedge-lined path to emerge onto a track. Climb the stile opposite, head diagonally across a sports field and on the far side cross a footbridge over Swindale Beck.

Turn left along a concrete path, left of a children's play area, and go through a gate onto a lane. The pubs and cafés of Market Brough are to the left; to return to the start, turn right into Church Brough and take the next right turn. ●

Durham – Riverside
and Woods

Start	Durham, Market Place
Distance	5 miles (8km)
Approximate time	2½ hours
Parking	Durham
Refreshments	Pubs and cafés at Durham, pub at Shincliffe Bridge, coffee shop at Botanic Garden near point Ⓓ
Ordnance Survey maps	Landranger 88 (Newcastle upon Tyne, Durham & Sunderland), Pathfinder 572, NZ 24/34 (Durham)

The opening and closing sections of this walk are along mainly wooded paths beside the River Wear. In between there is also much woodland walking, this time involving some relatively gentle climbing, with an opportunity to visit the University Botanic Garden. On the final stretch comes one of the greatest visual experiences in the country: the classic view of the towers and walls of Durham Cathedral and Castle rising majestically above the Wear.

There are few grander sights in Britain than that of Durham Cathedral and Castle, side by side on a wooded cliff within a horseshoe bend in the River Wear. Together they symbolise the twin powers of the medieval bishops of Durham – military as well as spiritual – for they were prince bishops, entrusted by the king with the task of protecting the area from Scottish invasions. Clustered around these two mighty structures and enclosed within the loop of the river are narrow and winding streets, lined with gracious old buildings, many of them now housing various university departments, which give the city a distinctly medieval feel.

Durham Cathedral is a masterpiece of Norman architecture, widely regarded as the finest in Europe. Founded in 995 as the last resting-place of St Cuthbert,

it was mostly constructed between 1093 and 1133, apart from the east end and central tower. Inside, the view is dominated by the majestic columns of the nave, characterised by the differing patterns on the stonework. The Galilee Chapel at the west end is the burial place of the Venerable Bede.

Although much altered and rebuilt by successive bishops, Durham Castle still retains the basic plan of the original Norman castle. The major alterations came after 1840 when it was given to the newly founded university and transformed into a residential college.

The walk starts in the Market Place. With your back to St Michael's Church, bear left along Saddler Street, at a fork take the left-hand, lower street to Elvet Bridge and descend steps to the left of the bridge to the river Ⓐ. Continue

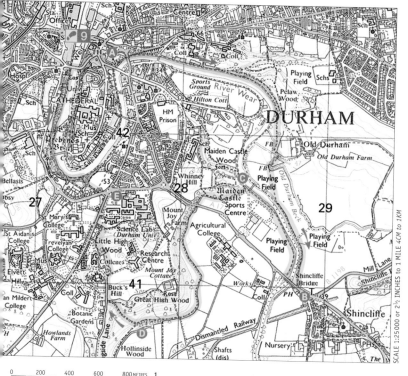

SCALE 1:25000 or 2½ INCHES to 1 MILE 4CM to 1KM

```
0      200    400    600   800 METRES  1
                                        KILOMETRES
                                        MILES
0     200    400   600 YARDS  ½
```

along the paved riverside path, passing under a modern road bridge; behind are grand views of the castle and cathedral.

After the paved section ends, the path continues through delightful riverside woods but, where the river bends to the right, keep ahead along a broad, straight path away from it. At a fork follow this path to the right between the brick supports of a former bridge and keep ahead to cross a footbridge over Old Durham Beck. Bear left across a playing-field and on the far side bear left to continue along the riverside path. If the path is overgrown, it may be easier to keep along the edge of the playing-field to the corner. Continue along a track beside the Wear, pass beside a metal gate and keep ahead to a road on the edge of Shincliffe, opposite the Rose Tree Inn **B**.

Turn right to cross Shincliffe Bridge and, at a public footpath sign, turn right onto a path and walk back along the other side of the river to the suspension footbridge – Maiden Castle Bridge – seen earlier when crossing the playing-field. Bear left across the field corner to go through a kissing-gate into Maiden Castle Wood **C** and turn left onto a path that keeps along the left-hand, inside edge of the trees. The thickly wooded hill to the right is the site of Maiden Castle, a prehistoric fort. At a fork, continue along the left-hand, lower path, which curves left to emerge onto a road.

Cross over and take the path opposite, which continues along the left-hand inside edge of Great High Wood, a delightful part of the walk with pleasant views across fields to the left. The path later bears slightly right uphill to a fork **D**. Take the right-hand, upper path, signed to University Botanic Garden, which climbs steadily through the trees and bears left at the top to emerge onto a lane via a stile. Turn right, and to the left is the entrance to the Botanic

Garden with its large variety of plants and colourful displays – well worth a visit.

Continue down the lane and, where it bears slightly left between university buildings, turn right – just before Fountains Hall – onto a track, pass beside a gate and turn left onto a path that crosses the end of two car parks. After the second car park, take the path ahead, which descends through Little High Wood, and at a fork continue down the left-hand narrower path that bears left, crosses a tarmac path and keeps ahead to a road. Turn right, at a crossroads turn left Ⓔ along Quarry Heads Lane and at a public footpath sign turn right onto a path that bears left along the edge of a playing-field, enters woodland and descends to a fork.

Take the right-hand, lower path, which bends left to join the riverside path. Now comes a spectacular and memorable finale as you follow this path through the woods beside the Wear, past Prebends Bridge and below Durham Cathedral and Castle, to Framwellgate Bridge. Climb steps beside the bridge, turn right over it and walk along Silver Street back to the Market Place.

Durham Castle – since 1836 occupied by University College Durham

Causey Arch and Beamish Woods

Start	Beamish Country Park, Causey Arch Picnic Area
Distance	5 miles (8km)
Approximate time	2½ hours
Parking	Causey Arch Picnic Area
Refreshments	Pub just before the end of the walk near point **G**
Ordnance Survey maps	Landranger 88 (Newcastle upon Tyne, Durham & Sunderland), Pathfinders 562, NZ 25/35 (Washington & Chester-le-Street) and 561, NZ 05/15 (Consett)

The walk takes you through a series of attractive woodlands, including the wooded gorge of Causey Burn, and there are many fine views over the surrounding countryside. Chief focal point and major historic site is the Causey Arch, one of the earliest engineering triumphs of the Industrial Revolution, which claims to be the oldest-surviving railway bridge in the world. The route also passes by the North of England Open Air Museum at Beamish, well worth a visit at the end of the walk.

Start by taking the path to the left of the toilet block, signposted to Causey Arch, which heads gently downhill through trees, below a railway embankment on the left. On reaching steps, turn right, in the 'Causey Arch via Gorge' direction, and descend into the gorge. Do not cross the first footbridge over Causey Burn but turn left alongside the burn and cross it at the second footbridge.

Continue through the wooded gorge, turn left over the next footbridge to recross the burn, climb steps, turn right and at the next bend Causey Arch is seen ahead. Cross the burn again, turn left to the arch, turn sharp right to climb steps beside it and turn left up to a T-junction **A**.

Turn left over the arch, both to enjoy the fine view and to see a replica wooden waggon and short length of wooden track on the other side. Causey Arch was built between 1725 and '26 to carry the wooden railway track across the gorge of the Causey Burn and is the oldest-surviving single-arch railway bridge in the world. The railway was constructed to carry coal from local mines to the River Tyne, but after an explosion at the nearby Tanfield Colliery in 1740 coal production declined and the waggonway across the arch closed in 1786. Iron rails and steam locomotives were later used on a new route but this closed in 1962. Part of that line is now used by a private company.

At the T-junction the route continues to the right through woodland. At a fork take the left-hand, lower path, signposted 'Top of Causey Gorge',

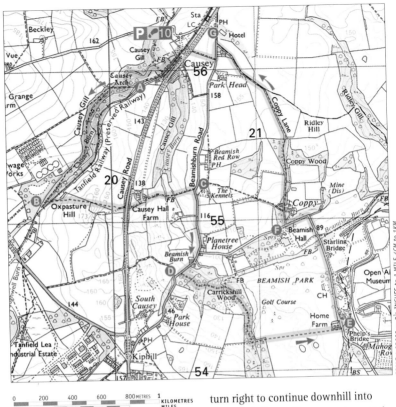

| 0 | 200 | 400 | 600 | 800 METRES | 1 | KILOMETRES |
| 0 | 200 | 400 | 600 YARDS | ½ | MILES |

which descends steps and keeps by the burn to a footbridge. Turn left over it **B** and turn left again on the other side, soon bearing right uphill away from the burn to a waymarked post. Turn sharp right here to go through a gate, cross a railway line, go through another gate, go up steps and follow a path around left and right bends to a stile. After climbing it, head gently uphill along the left edge of a field, pass through a fence gap on the brow, continue downhill along the edge of the next field and, at the bottom, turn left along a track to a road.

Cross over, descend steps, turn right along a narrow path and turn left over a stile. Bear slightly left to walk along the left-hand field edge, climb a stile in the corner, turn left and head down to pass through a gap between a wall corner and hedge. At a waymarked post,

turn right to continue downhill into woodland, descending more steps, and at the bottom keep ahead to cross a footbridge over a burn. Walk across grass to a stile at the bottom of a flight of steps, climb it and ascend those steps, keeping along the right edge of a field. Continue along the right field edge and turn right to climb a stile onto a lane **C**.

Turn right downhill and, at a public footpath sign about 200 yds (183m) after crossing a bridge over a burn, turn left **D** through an arch in a wall to enter Carrickshill Wood. Continue through the wood, bearing right on joining a broader and more clearly defined path. Ignoring a turn to the left, keep on the main path, which ascends and bears right again on joining another path to reach a T-junction. Turn left and at a fork immediately ahead, take the left-hand path along the right-hand, inside edge of the trees and climb a stile to exit from the wood.

Follow a straight track across Beamish Hall golf course, gently descending towards farm buildings on the far side and, on approaching the buildings, bear right off the track – following the waymarked posts – and walk across grass to steps in a brick wall and a sign 'Exit from Public Footpath'. Climb the steps into a paddock, go through a gate on the right, walk along a track beside Beamish Home Farm to a lane and turn left **E**. On the right are the grounds of the North of England Open Air Museum at Beamish, a revealing and imaginative re-creation of life in the North at the turn of the century. There is a lot to see and do here – farm, trams, railway station, coal mine and colliery village, etc – and a visit is recommended at the end of the walk.

Causey Arch

Head downhill along the lane, crossing a bridge over Beamish Burn and passing the entrance to Beamish Hall, and follow the lane around a left bend. At a public footpath sign to Causey Arch, turn right **F** onto a broad track (Coppy Lane) that heads steadily uphill and enters Coppy Wood. Go through a gate to leave the wood, continue across open country – with pleasant views on both sides – and, where the track bears left to a farm, keep ahead along a path, later emerging onto a drive and following it to a lane **G**. There is a pub just to the right.

Turn left and, at a public footpath sign, turn right over a stile and head gently downhill along the left edge of a field. Climb a stile in the bottom corner and turn left down to a road. Cross over and take the tarmac path opposite, passing under a railway bridge, to the car park. ●

Hamsterley Forest

Start	Hamsterley Forest Visitor Centre, signposted from Hamsterley village
Distance	5 miles (8km)
Approximate time	2½ hours
Parking	Hamsterley Forest
Refreshments	Café at Visitor Centre
Ordnance Survey maps	Landranger 92 (Barnard Castle & surrounding area), Outdoor Leisure 31 (North Pennines – Teesdale & Weardale)

This walk is essentially a circuit around both sides of the valley of Bedburn Beck, an undulating route with several ascents and descents that takes you beside sparkling becks and through mixed woodland, with some fine views over the forest from the higher points. The route is along well-waymarked forest trails and, apart from the last ¹/₄ mile (400m), you follow the orange arrows.

Hamsterley Forest, the largest in County Durham, comprises over 4,800 acres (2,000 ha) of mixed woodlands. It was formerly a hunting-estate and was purchased by the Forestry Commission in 1927 when the original conifer plantings were begun.

Start in front of the Visitor Centre by going through the kissing-gate opposite, descending steps and walking across the car park. Turn right onto a well-surfaced path, by a Bedburn Valley Walks sign, that runs beside the Bedburn Beck, bear left on joining another track and bear left again to cross a bridge over the beck **Ⓐ**.

Head steadily uphill, turn left at a T-junction and look out for where an orange waymark directs you to turn right off the track onto a steep, uphill path. On reaching a stony track, turn right, pass beside a metal barrier to a crossroads and keep ahead along a path, ascending gently to a T-junction. Turn

right downhill through dark conifers, turn left at a waymarked post, and the path bends right to continue down to a track. Turn left as far as a waymarked post – with both orange and yellow arrows – where you turn right and head quite steeply downhill through more dense conifers. Bear left on joining another path, continue down to a road, cross it and take the path opposite.

Turn left at a T-junction to cross a footbridge over a beck, turn right, descend steps and continue to another T-junction. Turn left along a path parallel to the road over to the right, and the path bends right to emerge onto the road to the right of a bridge **Ⓑ**. Turn left over the bridge, immediately turn right onto a path and bear right alongside a beck on meeting a track. At a crossroads to the right of a footbridge, turn right along a track that curves right and heads uphill. Where the main track turns left, keep ahead along a straight track that keeps along the right edge of trees and later starts to descend. From here there are fine open views to the right across to the thickly wooded slopes of the forest.

At a row of boulders, which act as a barrier between two converging tracks, bear right and continue more steeply downhill between gorse bushes to cross a footbridge over Ayhope Beck. Keep ahead

In Hamsterley Forest

up to the ruins of Metcalf's House, once a coaching inn, and at a waymarked post, turn right onto a path **C**. The path continues through the valley, sometimes beside the beck, to emerge onto a road to the left of the Green Man sculpture, a series of tall timber figures **D**.

Turn right – here leaving the orange-waymarked route – cross the beck and

turn left through Low Redford car park. Take the path that recrosses Ayhope Beck, at its confluence with Bedburn Beck, and continues between the beck on the right and fields on the left. The winding path briefly joins the road and then enters woodland.

At a crossings of ways **A**, keep ahead, here rejoining the outward route, and retrace your steps back to the start at the Visitor Centre. ●

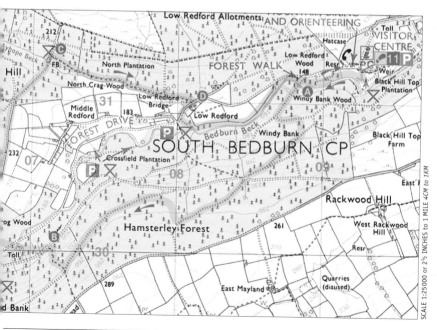

Around Dufton Pike

Start	Dufton
Distance	5½ miles (8.9km)
Approximate time	3 hours
Parking	Dufton
Refreshments	Pub in Dufton; snacks and soft drinks at the post office
Ordnance Survey maps	Landranger 91 (Appleby-in-Westmorland), Outdoor Leisure 19 (Howgill Fells & Upper Eden Valley) or 31 (North Pennines – Teesdale & Weardale)

Dufton Pike is the prominent, conically shaped hill (1,578ft/ 481m) north of Dufton. After a brief opening stretch through the steep-sided, wooded Dufton Ghyll or Gill, the route becomes a circuit of the lower slopes of the Pike, providing both pleasant and relatively easy walking and a succession of outstanding views of the surrounding, loftier peaks of the North Pennines. On the final leg – a gradual descent – the views extend across the gentler terrain of the Eden valley to the line of the Lakeland fells.

The attractive village of Dufton lies between two of the wildest, loneliest and most challenging stretches of the Pennine Way. Its pub, farms and red sandstone cottages, grouped around a wide green with a Victorian drinking-fountain, are overlooked by Dufton Pike.

Turn right out of the car park and immediately turn right again, at a public footpath sign to Ghyll, along a track. Curve left to reach a stile and, after climbing it, descend into the wooded valley. Since 1980 Dufton Ghyll has been owned by the Woodland Trust, who are attempting to re-establish its former woodland, largely felled by previous owners. At a public footpath sign to Mill Bridge and Brampton at the bottom, turn sharp right to cross a bridge over the beck and continue uphill to a fork.

Take the right-hand path, signposted to Mill Bridge, keep along the edge of the ghyll and, at the next fork, continue along the right-hand, lower path, which descends to the beck and turns right to recross it. Keep ahead through the trees, above Mill Beck on the left, and go through a gate onto a lane. Turn left to cross a bridge over the beck, follow the lane around a left-hand bend and, at a public footpath sign to St Cuthbert's Church, turn right Ⓐ over a stile and walk along the left-hand edge of a field, by a wire fence on the left.

Keep ahead at a fence corner, climb a stile at the next fence corner and continue along the bottom, inside edge of sloping woodland to another stile. Climb it, turn right to cross a tributary beck, go through a gate, continue beside the beck and climb a stone stile onto a lane just to the left of Church Bridge. Ahead, above the beck and cradled by high fells, is the 18th-century St Cuthbert's Church.

Turn left along a narrow lane that curves right and continues into the

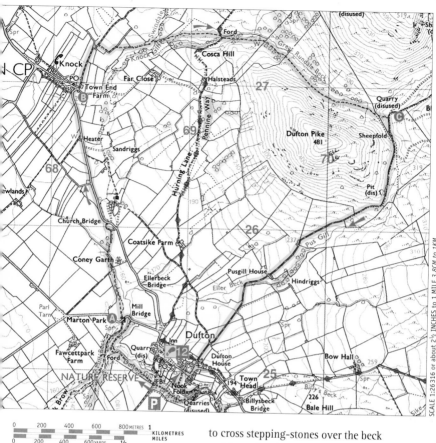

0	200	400	600	800 METRES	1
					KILOMETRES
					MILES

0	200	400	600 YARDS	½

hamlet of Knock. At a public footpath sign to Cross Fell, where the lane turns sharp left **B**, keep ahead through a farmyard and along an enclosed track. Ahead is Knock Pike and to the right is Dufton Pike. At a fork, take the right-hand track and, at a footpath sign 'Dufton via Back of Pike', turn right over a stile and walk along the right-hand edge of a field. After climbing a stile, continue along an enclosed track that turns left and heads gently uphill.

At the top of the rise, turn right over a stile, walk along the left-hand field edge, turn left over a stile in the corner and keep ahead, by an old hedgebank on the right, above the steep-sided, wooded valley of Swindale Beck. At a waymarked post by the end of a short section of walling, bear right downhill

to cross stepping-stones over the beck and keep ahead to a stile. Climb it and take the path ahead, which climbs through trees to another stile. Cross it, continue across a field, keeping parallel to Great Rundale Beck, climb a stone stile on the far side and turn right to first cross a small clapper bridge and then climb stone stile to a T-junction.

Turn left onto an uphill track, contouring along the lower slopes of Dufton Pike to a stone stile. Climb it, keep ahead above the beck on the left, over another stile and across the slopes of the Pike, curving gradually right and heading gently uphill all the while. Eventually, bear slightly left and climb a stone stile to a T-junction.

Turn right **C** along a track to begin the descent back to Dufton. The track winds downhill through a series of gates to emerge onto a road by Dufton Hall Farm. Bear right and follow the road around a right-hand bend to the start. ●

Kirkby Stephen and Nateby

Start	Kirkby Stephen
Distance	6½ miles (10.5km)
Approximate time	3½ hours
Parking	Kirkby Stephen
Refreshments	Pubs and cafés at Kirkby Stephen, pub at Nateby
Ordnance Survey maps	Landranger 91 (Appleby-in-Westmorland), Outdoor Leisure 19 (Howgill Fells & Upper Eden Valley)

After an attractive opening stretch beside the River Eden, the route continues into the village of Nateby and then heads gently uphill out of the valley, giving fine views of the North Pennines and Howgill Fells. The last 2 miles (3.2km) are on the Coast to Coast Path – a gradual descent into Kirkby Stephen with views of the town nestling below in the Eden valley. All the climbs on this walk are gradual and relatively easy.

Kirkby Stephen is a long, narrow town situated on the west bank of the River Eden. The hub of the town is the Market Square, where the walk begins. With your back to the Butter Market and medieval church – the latter is one of the largest and grandest in Cumbria – turn left along Stoneshot, following signs to River Eden and Frank's Bridge. Continue along a tarmac path between high walls that bends right and, at another sign to River Eden and Frank's Bridge, turn left down steps and cross the bridge over the Eden.

Turn right onto a riverside path and, after going through a kissing-gate, turn right across the grass Ⓐ and keep alongside the tree-lined river, by a wire fence on the right. In the corner of a meadow, cross a footbridge over a tributary beck and follow the path into woodland, bending right to emerge from the trees. Continue along a narrow, enclosed path for ½ mile (800m), fording a beck, and turn right onto a wider path after

crossing a disused railway bridge. At a fork, take the right-hand path, cross a bridge over a beck and head up to a road.

Keep ahead into Nateby, passing the small village green, and at a public

footpath sign to Wharton Hall turn right over a stone stile **B**. Walk along an enclosed path, go through a metal gate and keep straight ahead across a field. Go through a gate, bear slightly left across the next field, go through a fence gap and descend to the riverbank again, where you go through a kissing-gate. Follow the Eden around a left-hand bend, turn right to cross a foot-bridge over it and keep ahead uphill to go through a gate.

Cross a tarmac track, go through a gate opposite and – ignoring various bridleway signs – keep straight ahead uphill, looking out for a stone stile in the wall in front. Climb it, keep ahead across a field towards a railway bridge, climb another stile, continue to a yellow waymark and turn left alongside a wall below the railway embankment. Turn right to go through a gate and pass under the railway bridge, bear slightly

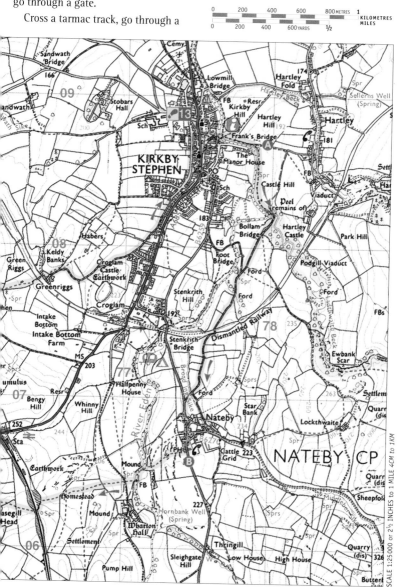

right across a field, go through another gate and keep in the same direction across the next field to a metal gate. After going through it, bear left towards a farm, go through a metal gate into the farmyard, turn first left and then right to go through another metal gate and continue along a track to a road.

Turn right, at a T-junction turn left and take the first lane on the right **G**, signposted to Waitby and Smardale. After ¾ mile (1.2km), turn right onto a lane signposted to Waitby **D** and, at a public footpath sign to Kirkby Stephen, turn right over a stone stile, here joining the Coast to Coast Path. Head diagonally downhill across a field towards a wall on the far side, bear right alongside the wall and, at a corner, turn left and keep ahead to pass under a railway bridge again. Keep ahead across the next field, bearing gradually right to climb a stone stile in the far corner.

Now bear slightly left and, as you head downhill, a grand view opens up over of the Eden valley with the tower of Kirkby Stephen church visible. After climbing a stile, continue through a shallow valley down to a stone stile, climb it, walk along the right-hand field edge, go through a gate and pass between the supports of a former railway bridge to a metal gate. Turn right in front of a barn, go through another metal gate and turn left between farm buildings.

Continue along a winding, enclosed track – which later becomes tarmacked – into Kirkby Stephen, emerging onto a road. Keep along it and, opposite a footpath sign on the left to 'Car Park', turn right along an alley which leads back into the Market Square. ●

Frank's Bridge over the River Eden at Kirkby Stephen

Lazonby and Kirkoswald

Start	Lazonby, Bridge End car park, by Eden Bridge
Distance	6½ miles (10.5km). Shorter version 5½ miles (8.9km)
Approximate time	3½ hours (3 hours for the shorter walk)
Parking	Bridge End car park at Lazonby
Refreshments	Pubs at Lazonby, pubs at Kirkoswald
Ordnance Survey maps	Landrangers 86 (Haltwhistle & Brampton, Bewcastle & Alston), 90 (Penrith & Keswick, Ambleside) and 91 (Appleby-in-Westmorland), Outdoor Leisure 5 (The English Lakes – North Eastern area)

On this easy-paced walk in the Eden valley, there are a series of fine views across the valley to the moorlands of the North Pennines and the outline of the Lakeland fells. There is pleasant walking across fields, along lanes and by woodlands and, towards the end, an attractive stretch beside the River Eden. The route passes through the village of Kirkoswald, which has an interesting and secluded church. The shorter route omits an initial short loop around the village of Lazonby.

If doing the shorter route, walk down to Eden Bridge **C** *and start from there.*

For the full walk, turn left out of the car park and walk up the road into the village. By the Victorian church, turn right **A** along a lane signposted to Baronwood and Armathwaite and after nearly ½ mile (800m) turn right over a stone stile, at a public footpath sign to Eden Bridge Park **B**. Walk along the left-hand edge of a field, cross a beck and, where the field edge turns left, keep straight ahead, turning right when you see a stile in a fence. Climb it, keep ahead to climb a stile onto the road near the start and turn left **C** to cross the 18th-century bridge over the River Eden, here picking up the shorter route.

Continue along the road into Kirkoswald, curving right and passing the entrance to St Oswald's Church to reach a junction. The church, dedicated to an early king of Northumbria, lies at the base of a conical hill overlooking meadows and is unusual in that it has a detached belfry on the hill above. It is a short but wide building with a fine Norman nave.

The main part of Kirkoswald, an attractive village with two pubs, is to the left of the road junction; the route continues ahead, in the Glassonby and Alston direction, to a fork, where you take the left-hand lane, signposted to Park Head and Alston. At a public footpath sign to Glassonby, turn right over a stile **D**, keep along the right-hand field edge and continue along a tree-lined track to a stile. To the left are the scanty remains of Kirkoswald Castle, founded in the 12th century and burnt – as was the village – by Scottish armies after the Battle of Bannockburn in 1314. However, its present ruinous

Eden Bridge at Lazonby

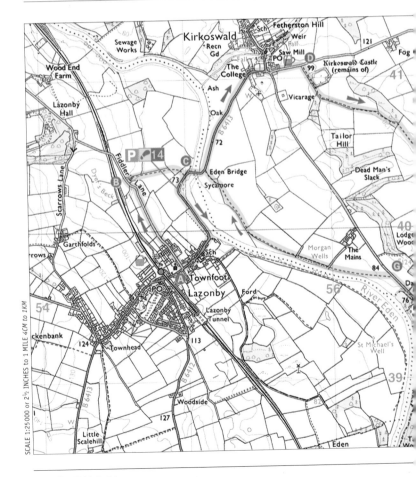

state is more the result of its stones being pilfered by local people to build farmhouses and cottages.

After climbing the stile, keep ahead by the right-hand field edge to a way-marked post, turn left and walk gently uphill along a grassy ledge above the field on the left, continuing to a gate in the field corner. Turn right – through the wooden gate, not the metal one beside it – and walk along a fence-lined track, by woodland on the left, bearing slightly right to a gate. Go through, keep ahead across the next field towards trees and, on the far side, descend to climb a stile. Walk along the right-hand field edge, by woodland on the right, and after about 100 yds (91m), climb a stile in a fence and continue along the left-hand edge of the wood. Climb a stile to emerge from it, keep ahead to go through a gate, head across the field corner to a waymarked post and continue along the right-hand field edge, by woodland again on the right.

Go through a gate, keep ahead towards a farm, joining a track, and go through a gate into the farmyard. Turn right through another gate and continue along a tarmac track to a lane **E**. Turn right, descending to cross Glassonby Beck, follow the lane to the right and continue up into Glassonby. At a junction, bear right through the village and, at a small triangular green in front of the next junction, turn right, in the Kirkoswald and Lazonby direction **F**. The road winds gradually downhill to Daleraven Bridge and about 200 yds (183m) beyond it, turn left through a gate, at a public footpath sign to Eden Bridge **G**.

Walk along the left-hand field edge, bearing right to continue along an embankment above the River Eden, and climb a stile in the field corner. Keep along a track by the river, go through a gate, and continue along the track, bearing slightly right away from the river to go through another gate. Continue by the left-hand field edge, turn left over a stile and keep by the right-hand field edge to climb a stile to the right of Eden Bridge. Turn left over it to return to the start.

| 0 | 200 | 400 | 600 | 800 METRES | 1 |
| 0 | 200 | 400 | 600 YARDS | ½ | KILOMETRES / MILES |

Marsden Rock and Whitburn

Start	Marsden Bay, between South Shields and Whitburn
Distance	7 miles (11.3km)
Approximate time	3½ hours
Parking	Marsden Bay, car park about 300 yds (274m) south of the junction of the A183 (coast road) and the A1300 – there are other car parks nearby
Refreshments	Pub at Marsden Rock, tearoom at Souter Lighthouse
Ordnance Survey maps	Landranger 88 (Newcastle upon Tyne, Durham & Sunderland), Pathfinder 550, NZ 45/46 (Sunderland & Whitburn (Tyne & Wear))

Initially the walk heads inland, climbing gently over the modest Cleadon Hills (272ft/83m) and then descending to the attractive coastal village of Whitburn. From here the rest of the route hugs the coast, keeping along the top of low cliffs and passing several stacks and rock arches. Apart from distant views of Tyneside and Wearside and the proximity of suburban South Shields, the rural nature of this walk does little to indicate that this was once an industrial area, but the route passes by a disused quarry, abandoned limekilns and along the edge of Whitburn Coastal Park, reclaimed from the site of a former colliery. Because of the instability of the cliffs, it is important not to cross the barrier while walking along the coast path.

Part of the coast path runs alongside a firing range. If the range is being used – indicated by red flags flying or lights showing – use the diversion described in the route directions at point **F**.

Begin by heading across the grass to the coast path and turn right along it to the huge limestone stack of Marsden Rock, renowned for its seabird colonies. Until recently it was the most impressive arch on this stretch of coast but the arch collapsed a few years ago in a storm.

From the rock, bear right back to the road, cross it and, at a public footpath sign just beyond the end of a caravan site, turn right onto an enclosed path **A**. The path bends first left and then right, heads gently uphill, between a golf course on the left and the caravan site on the right, passes beside a barrier and keeps ahead to a road. Turn left and at a public footpath sign to Cleadon Park, turn right and continue uphill. To the right are a disused quarry and views across South Shields to the mouth of the Tyne. Keep beside a combination of hedge, fence and wall on the left and, on reaching a public footpath sign, turn

left over a stone stile in the wall **B**.

Walk in a straight line across the golf course, heading towards a wall on the left and aiming for a point just to the left of a tall brick tower, a water pumping station. On the far side of the

course, keep ahead along a path to go through a metal gate and continue, by a wall on the left, to a kissing-gate. Go through, and the path now bears left and continues over the Cleadon Hills, by a wall on the left, passing the disused Cleadon Windmill, built in the early 19th century. The mouth of the Wear and Sunderland can be seen straight ahead.

Marsden Rock

After passing the windmill, the route continues gently downhill. At a fork take the left-hand path to a stile. Climb it, keep ahead to climb another one, and the path – which might be overgrown at this point – bends right between fields. Follow it around left- and right-hand bends to a stile, climb it and keep ahead along an enclosed path to another stile. After climbing that, turn left onto a straight track along the left-hand edge of fields, go through a gate, continue between farm buildings and on along a tarmac drive to a road on the edge of Whitburn **C**.

Turn right, at a T-junction turn right again, take the first turning on the left – Sandy Chare – and at the next junction turn left again **D** along Whitburn's attractive village green, lined by handsome 18th- and 19th-century houses. Bear right along a tarmac path across a corner of the green, turn right along Church Lane, passing the mainly 13th-century church, and where the lane ends keep ahead beside a barrier and continue along an enclosed tarmac track, beside a park on the left. Go through a gate onto the coast road **E**, cross over, take the road opposite and at a public footpath sign bear right to join the coast path. Follow the path along the top of the low, crumbly cliffs to the kissing-gate at the start of the Whitburn Firing Range. If firing is not in progress, go through and keep ahead along the edge of the range to pass beside a metal barrier at its far corner **G**.

If lights or red flags are showing to indicate that firing is taking place, it is necessary to make a diversion inland. About 200 yds (183m) before the kissing-gate **F**, follow a cycle track to the left, go through a barrier and keep ahead along a road to the main coast road. Turn right and after just over ¹/₂ mile (800m), turn right down Fern Avenue. Turn left along Rose Crescent, turn right at a crossroads into Marsden Avenue and, where it ends, climb a stile and walk along a straight track towards the sea. The path turns first left then right, left and right again and reaches the coast path at point **G**. Turn left to rejoin it.

Now comes the most spectacular part of the coast walk as the path keeps by a wall on the left bordering the Whitburn Coastal Park, an area of grassland reclaimed from the site of the former Whitburn Colliery. Part of it is a nature reserve. Ahead are Souter Lighthouse and Lizard Point and on this stretch of coast there are several stacks and rock arches. Pass beside a barrier to the right of the lighthouse, built in 1871 and now open to the public, and continue across The Leas, a National Trust area of grassland, cliffs and beaches. On the other side of the road are the imposing remains of the 19th-century Marsden Limekilns.

Continue along the coast path to Marsden Rock and on to the start. ●

Auckland Park, Escomb and the River Wear

Start	Bishop Auckland
Distance	7½ miles (12.1km) Two shorter versions of 3½ miles (5.6km) and 4 miles (6.4km)
Approximate time	4 hours (2 hours for each of the shorter walks)
Parking	Bishop Auckland
Refreshments	Pubs and cafés at Bishop Auckland, pub at Escomb
Ordnance Survey maps	Landrangers 92 (Barnard Castle & surrounding area) and 93 (Middlesbrough, Darlington & Hartlepool), Pathfinders 580, NZ 12/13 (Crook & West Auckland), 581, NZ 23/33 (Spennymoor & Coxhoe) and 590, NZ 22/32 (Newton Aycliffe)

There is considerable historic interest on this figure-of-eight walk, centred on the town of Bishop Auckland. The first half is essentially a circuit of the boundary of Auckland Park, once the deer park of Auckland Castle, the palace of the bishops of Durham. The second half takes you along the banks of the River Wear, under a massive Victorian viaduct and across delightful meadows, to the little Saxon church at Escomb. The route can obviously be split into two separate, shorter walks. On the second part of the walk, there is one short, muddy and uneven section.

The large Market Place in Bishop Auckland is dominated by the handsome Victorian town hall, built in 1862, and adjoining it is the almost contemporary St Anne's Church. Leading off from the Market Place is the 18th-century gatehouse to Auckland Castle, since the 12th century the seat of the powerful Prince Bishops of Durham. Although much altered and restored, the castle has some interesting features and is particularly noted for the magnificent chapel, converted from a medieval, aisled hall in the 17th century.

The full walk and both the shorter alternatives start in the Market Place, in front of the town hall.

If doing the second part of the walk only – along the river to Escomb – pass to the left of the town hall, take the first turning on the left and descend steeply to the river, joining the full walk at point ⓓ.

For the first part of the walk only – the circuit of Auckland Park – and the full walk, pass to the right of the town hall, by St Anne's Church, and turn right in front of the entrance to Auckland Castle. Bear left at the junction ahead, in the Spennymoor and Durham direction, and at a public footpath sign turn left up steps to a stile ⓐ. Climb it

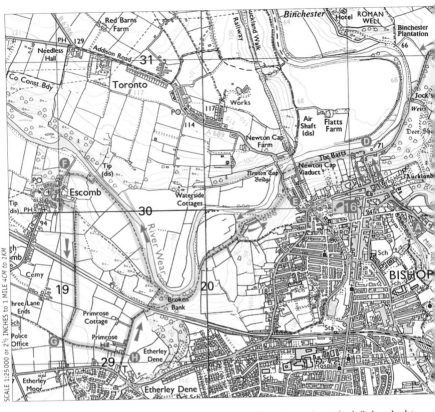

and take the path ahead to climb another one.

Head uphill by the left-hand edge of a field, alongside the boundary wall of Auckland Park – part of which is now Bishop Auckland golf course – and climb a stile in the top corner. Cross the drive leading to the golf club, keep ahead along an enclosed path, climb a stile and continue along the left-hand edge of three fields, climbing two more stiles. After climbing another stile in the bottom corner of the third field, turn left **B** onto a straight, flat and well-surfaced track. This was formerly part of the railway line between Bishop Auckland and Spennymoor.

At first the track runs along the top of a low embankment and then continues through a wooded cutting. After passing under the first bridge, turn right up steps, turn left at the top, climb a stile and turn left to cross the second bridge **C**. Walk along a left-hand field edge

and continue along the left-hand edge of a succession of fields and over a series of stiles, with the deer park over to the left, finally bearing left to climb a stile onto a lane. Bear left alongside the River Wear, cross a bridge over the little River Gaunless by its confluence with the Wear and continue along the lane to where it turns left **D**. Ahead are fine views of Newton Cap Viaduct, and Auckland Castle can be seen on the hill to the left.

If only doing the circuit of Auckland Park, turn left and follow the lane steeply uphill to the start.

For the full walk, turn right along a tarmac drive, follow it around a left-hand bend and, where it ends, keep ahead across riverside meadows, passing under the viaduct. The imposing Newton Cap Viaduct was constructed between 1856 and '57 to carry the railway over the River Wear. It was closed in 1968 and has subsequently been

converted into a road bridge. Continue to a bridge, climb steps in front of it up to a road, turn left uphill and take the first turning on the right **E**. Keep along the left-hand edge of a grassy picnic area, passing to the left of Bishop Auckland Rugby Club, and where the road ends at a small car park climb the stone stile immediately in front.

Keep beside the river, following it around a right-hand bend across the trees, gorse and scrub of Broken Bank. At this point the route is uneven and likely to be muddy and there are several paths but the landmark to make for is a bench with yellow waymarks. From here you continue along a clearer path to a stile. After climbing it, the path descends and turns left to reach a foot-bridge. Turn right over it, turn left and now comes a most attractive part of the walk as you continue across a succession of meadows beside the Wear, climbing a series of stiles. After climbing the stile at the far end of the last meadow, turn left along a path that bends right to another stile. Climb it, keep along the left-hand field edge, climb a stile, continue along a path and

bear left along a road **F** into the village of Escomb.

The road curves right to the tiny, narrow Saxon church, which is a rare survival and one of the finest examples of its kind in England. It was built in the late 7th century, and some of the stones are thought to be Roman, probably taken from the nearby fort of Vinovia (Binchester).

Turn left in front of the church and take the first turning on the left (Bede Close). Where the road bends right, keep ahead along a tarmac path, climb a stile and continue between wire fences to climb another one. At a footpath post just ahead, turn right, in the direction of the public bridleway, and head uphill across the field to a stile. Climb it, continue by the right-hand field edge, climb a stile in the corner and keep ahead to go through a gate. Climb another stile and cross a railway bridge. Keep ahead over a stile and along the right-hand edge of a field, go through a gap, continue along the right-hand edge of the next field and climb a stile in the top corner.

Turn left **G** along an enclosed path, by garden fences on the right, and continue along the right-hand edge of a field to a stile. Climb it, keep ahead along a gravel path to the end of a road and turn left **H** along a broad track. After passing the last of the houses, the track narrows, becomes enclosed between hedges and heads gently down-hill, bearing right to a stile. Climb it, continue down to cross a railway line, climb another stile and immediately turn right onto a path that heads down through the trees and gorse of Broken Bank again to reach the waymarked bench passed earlier.

Here you pick up the outward route and retrace your steps to the corner of the lane **D**. Keep ahead steeply uphill to return to the Market Place. ●

Egglestone Abbey, Paradise and the Meeting of the Waters

Start	Egglestone Abbey, near Barnard Castle
Distance	7 miles (11.3km)
Approximate time	3 hours
Parking	Car park by abbey ruins
Refreshments	Pub at Whorlton
Ordnance Survey maps	Landranger 92 (Barnard Castle & surrounding area), Outdoor Leisure 31 (Teesdale), Pathfinder 599, NZ 01/11 (Barnard Castle & Gainford)

This is a straight-forward walk beside the River Tees as it flows majestically by crags and rocks through woodland and farmland. There are monastic ruins, an ancient tower and a grand country-house along the route, and on every inch of the path you are treading in the footsteps of great painters and writers from the Romantic age.

Leave the car park at Egglestone Abbey and head back down the access road beside the ruins. The abbey was built in a charming position overlooking the Tees, where it is joined by the waters of the Thorsgill Beck. It was a Premonstratensian foundation of the late 12th century, colonised by the monks from Easby Abbey, near Richmond. After the dissolution it was converted into a

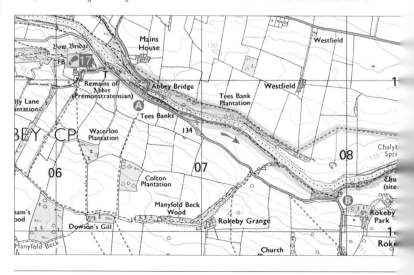

manor-house, but enough of its fabric survives to make this still a holy spot.

After the cattle-grid, turn right along Abbey Lane, cross the road at Abbey Bridge and go through the gate into the wood where the footpath sign points to the Meeting of the Waters and Whorlton 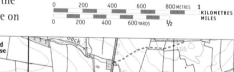. The newly made path zigzags down to the river, which here flows swiftly through a long, limestone gorge, a popular place for white-water canoeists. Follow the path down the gorge with crags rearing up on either side, then cross the stepping-stones at Manyfold Beck and climb the steep steps into the field high above the river. Stay close beside the fence to the left and climb the sturdy wooden stile into Paradise, the delightful name of this ancient woodland. In addition to commonplace north-country broadleaf trees, you will see limes, yews and Spanish chestnuts growing here. Follow the path as it meanders through Paradise, then go through the gate and turn left into Mortham Lane Ⓑ.

Across parkland to the right there are glimpses of Rokeby Hall, a grand country-house built in 1731 by Sir Thomas Robinson, who was a noted amateur architect and patron of the arts. Sir Walter Scott stayed there on working holidays to write his novels and poetry, and the painters Turner and Cotman recorded all of Teesdale's beauty spots while based at Rokeby. One of Turner's greatest landscapes is of the Meeting of the Waters, where the turbulent Greta joins the broader Tees Ⓒ. This scene remained unchanged from Turner's visit until the floods caused by the hurricane in October 1987 rearranged the bedrock in an awesome demonstration of elemental force.

Follow the lane right and then turn left over Dairy Bridge; look down into the peat-brown waters of the Greta rushing through the narrow limestone gorge. At the cattle-grid there is a helpful footpath map on the gate. Follow the drive, turning right up the hill to Mortham Tower, originally a 14th-century peel or tower house built to protect against border raiders. Turn left off the drive Ⓓ and take the grassy path along the ridge, crossing three stiles standing beside field gates and keep the neat hedge on the right. There are cultivation terraces in the broad fields running down to the river, with

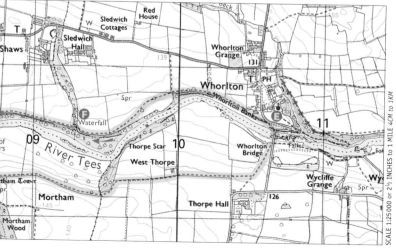

Egglestone Abbey

prominent sandstone cliffs beyond. There are several large pinkish boulders beside the path – these are glacial erratics of Shap granite, transported here from the Lake District by glaciers in the last Ice Age.

Cross the cart bridge and bear left round the fence beside the wood, then turn right to walk the headland path alongside the wall past the ruins of West Thorpe. This is rich arable farmland, and the transition from pasture to plough marks the boundary between hill farming and lowland farming. Go through the metal field gate, then bear left to the stile in the roadside wall some fifty paces from the southern end of Whorlton Bridge. Cross the bridge, which is of a remarkable suspension design built in 1831, and turn left by the toll cottage on the north bank to climb the long flight of steps. At the top a footpath sign points left, but if you are in need of refreshment at this point you must divert up the road to the Bridge Inn, which overlooks the village green.

Back at the footpath sign **E**, follow the grassy path back updale with the Tees always in sight to your left. There are numerous stiles and gates, but the route is straightforward until Sledwich Gill **F**. Here a flight of steps leads down to a footbridge across the beck,

followed by a steep ascent to more stiles and gates. The woodland on your left, Crossberry Plantation, is now owned by Durham County Council, and the intention is to divert the footpath to follow a route through the wood and nearer to the river, to the Meeting of the Waters, where Turner painted near the Chalybeate Spring, complete with an angler in the foreground, and red iron-stains on the surrounding bedrock clearly identify the scene.

At the time of writing, stay on the public footpath that bears away slightly to the right **G** before turning left, and proceeds along the field edges outside Tees Bank Plantation, before entering the wood for a short section. Eventually the path crosses a field to emerge via a stone stile and steps onto the road just north of Abbey Bridge. Durham County Council have also purchased Tees Bank Plantation, and again the long-term objective is to create an attractive riverside/woodland walk as part of the Teesdale Way. Turn left and follow the road down to cross Abbey Bridge, a single lofty arch built in 1773, vaulting from crag to crag with embattled parapets above and the cascading river beneath, then turn right and finally fork left to return to the abbey. ●

Cauldron Snout

Start	Langdon Beck
Distance	6½ miles (10.5km)
Approximate time	3½ hours
Parking	At the point where the Cauldron Snout footpath leaves Langdon Beck to Cow Green Reservoir road, beyond the track to Widdy Bank Farm
Refreshments	From 19.00 only or booked parties during the day at the Langdon Beck Hotel, tel. 01833 622267, ½ mile (800m) from the starting point
Ordnance Survey maps	Landrangers 91 (Appleby-in-Westmorland) and 92 (Barnard Castle & surrounding area), Outdoor Leisure 31 (Teesdale)

There is easy walking for the greater part of this route but it must be emphasised that great care should be taken on the section below Falcon Clints, where, as the name suggests, the path is through a scatter of boulders and loose stone. Arrival below the waterfall is a wonderful reward for the scramble, and this must be the most satisfying way to visit Cauldron Snout, which is at its most impressive after a night of heavy rain. Be careful of the many old mine shafts in the area, some of which may still be open and thus attractive to dogs or children who stray from the path. Parts may not be enjoyable for those who suffer from vertigo.

The path follows the track, which twists and turns towards white-painted Widdy Bank Farm **Ⓐ**, now the regional head-quarters of English Nature.

The farmhouse garden grows brave flowers and vegetables for such a windswept spot (Upper Teesdale has 20.8 days of snow in an average January and its summer temperatures are akin to those of Reykjavík).

Go through the farmyard and a meadow to join a riverside track that passes by an Upper Teesdale Nature Reserve notice-board. Perhaps in recognition of this the numerous grouse seem ridiculously tame.

The walking on this stretch – Holmwath – is perfect. Springy grass underfoot and grand scenery all about. All too soon, however, the terrain changes as the path becomes narrow and closer to the river. Rocks and boulders slow progress though long runs of slatted boards give relief. These allow the grass to reinstate itself in boggy places where the path has become eroded. No expense has been spared in covering the path across the marshy land of Lingy Holm **Ⓑ** with these walkways.

Take great care over the huge boulders as the riverside path nears the

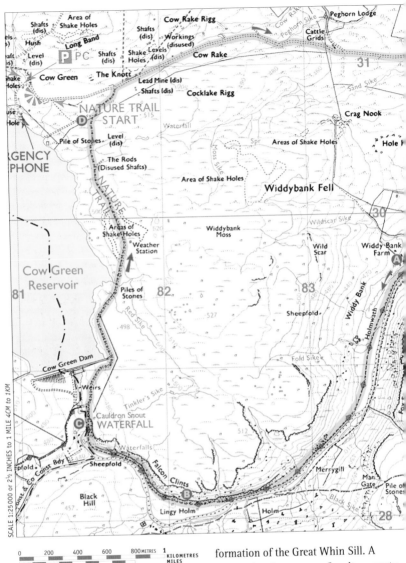

SCALE 1:25 000 or 2½ INCHES to 1 MILE 4CM to 1KM

0	200	400	600	800 METRES	1

KILOMETRES
MILES

0	200	400	600 YARDS	½

meeting of the Maize Beck with the Tees. Stone-built cattle-shelters overlook the two streams. The noise of the waterfall can now be clearly heard – and if there has been recent rain its appearance is no anticlimax. Because you are so close to its turbulent waters the spectacle is even more impressive than High Force. The waterfall **C** owes its existence to a geological event that took place 295 million years ago: the formation of the Great Whin Sill. A great volcanic upsurge of molten quartz dolerite intruded into the various strata lying above, completely changing the composition of the various rocks as it flowed sideways and upwards, and creating the whinstone crag over which the water cascades. The characteristic six-sided blocks, which can be seen as you climb the rocks by the side of the waterfall, were formed by the rapid cooling of the dolerite intrusion into a crystalline form.

The concrete dam comes into view

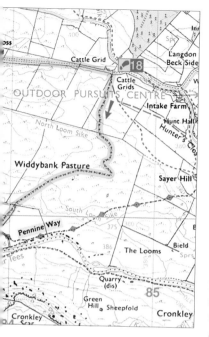

various stops on the Nature Conservancy's Widdybank Fell Nature Trail. A booklet on this may be bought at the car park at Cow Green.

Another by-product of the Whin Sill metamorphosis was the creation of sugar limestone. This supports a remarkable range of plants, among them the spring gentian (*Gentiana verna*). This is its only habitat in mainland Britain.

A further result of the igneous intrusion was the creation of minerals, the most valuable being barytes and lead. Cow Green was one of a number of mines that flourished here until about the end of the 19th century. Reminders of the mining industry are still to be seen on the landscape here and on other parts of Teesdale and Alston Moor.

When the path divides ⓓ take the fork to the right to join the road from Cow Green Reservoir car park. It is about 2 miles (3.2km) back to the starting point from here along the road. This is enjoyable as the scenery remains superb and there are no demanding gradients.

near the top. There is a dizzy view down from here – not enjoyable for those who suffer from vertigo.

Join the road leading to Birkdale and turn right, thus leaving the Pennine Way. You will soon be walking by the shore of the Cow Green Reservoir. The numbered posts that you see are the

Cauldron Snout

Talkin Tarn and Gelt Woods

Talkin Tarn and Gelt Woods

Start	Talkin Tarn Country Park, signposted from the A69 to the south of Brampton
Distance	7 miles (11.3km)
Approximate time	3½ hours
Parking	Talkin Tarn Country Park
Refreshments	Café at Country Park, pubs at Talkin, hotel at south end of Talkin Tarn
Ordnance Survey maps	Landranger 86 (Haltwhistle & Brampton, Bewcastle & Alston), Pathfinder 558, NY 45/55 (Carlisle (East) & Castle Carrock)

There are three main focal points on this varied walk in the countryside just to the east of Carlisle. First comes a highly attractive and tranquil tarn that is the centrepiece of a country park. Second, there is a spectacular walk through the thickly wooded gorge of the River Gelt. Third, the route passes through the pleasant and quiet village of Talkin. The walk ends with a relaxing stroll beside Talkin Tarn. Apart from some 'up and down' walking through the gorge, with some rocky paths in places, this is an easy and well-waymarked route, with no steep ascents or difficult stretches.

From the car park, walk down to the tarn and turn left along its wooded shores to the Boathouse Tearoom. After passing in front of the tearoom, turn left beside it into the trees and follow the path as it bends right to continue along a tree-lined avenue to a public footpath sign to Brampton Hill Road. Turn left here over a stile, walk along the left-hand edge of a field, later continuing along a track, and go through a metal kissing-gate onto a lane Ⓐ.

Turn left along the lane for just under ½ mile (800m), crossing a railway line, and at a T-junction keep ahead along a track, at a public footpath sign to Brampton and Gelt Woods. Descend gently to go through a metal gate, keep ahead to pass in front of a farm and at a public footpath sign to Gelt Woods, turn left onto another track Ⓑ. At a fork by a farm, take the right-hand track towards a barn and turn right through a metal gate in front of it. The path bears left beside it and continues by a wall on the left to a stile.

Climb it to enter Gelt Woods and, at a T-junction of paths, turn left down through the trees to a fork. Take the left-hand path, signposted to Middle Gelt, and continue along the side of the thickly wooded gorge high above the river. The path is an undulating one – sometimes passing below sheer rock faces – and at the next fork, take the left-hand, upper path, later descending steps to cross a footbridge over a

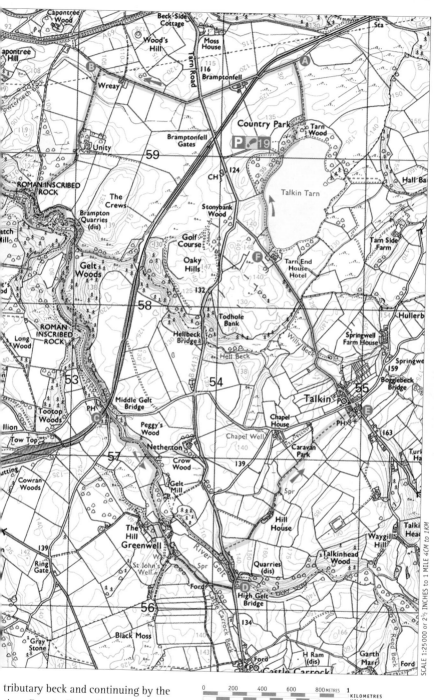

tributary beck and continuing by the river. Eventually go through a gate to emerge onto a road by Middle Gelt Bridge and the Victorian railway viaduct.

Turn right over the bridge and immediately turn left **C** along a lane,

signposted to Greenwell, passing under the viaduct. At a public footpath sign to Greenwell, turn left over a stile and continue through trees beside the River

Beside Talkin Tarn

Gelt to a stile. After climbing it, keep along the edge of riverside meadows, climb another stile at their far end and follow a path across rough grassland to emerge onto the lane again via a stone stile. Turn left through the hamlet of Greenwell, and at the end of the lane, keep ahead along a track in front of houses to a metal gate.

Go through, continue along a track, go through another gate, cross a foot-bridge over a beck and keep ahead to a road **D**. Turn left, cross High Gelt Bridge and, about 200 yds (183m) beyond it, turn right over a stile, at a public footpath sign to Talkin. Head diagonally uphill across a field towards a wall on the left, turn left through a metal gate in the wall and walk along an enclosed track to a farm. Pass through the farmyard, continue along a track and, after going through another metal gate, bear left to continue along the left-hand edge of the next two fields, going through two more metal gates.

Keep ahead across the next two fields, going through two gates, cross a track to a waymarked post and continue along a path to a stone stile. Climb it and turn left beside the Blacksmiths Arms to a road junction in Talkin village **E**. Near the pub is the 19th-century church, built in an imitation Norman style. Keep ahead along a lane, in the Talkin Tarn and Brampton direction, and just beyond the Tarn End House Hotel, turn right through a kissing-gate **F** to re-enter the country park and head down to the tarn.

Now comes a most pleasant and attractive finale as you turn left and follow a path across meadows and through woodland beside it – passing through two kissing-gates – to return to the start.

Wolsingham and the Weardale Way

Start	Wolsingham
Distance	7½ miles (12.1km)
Approximate time	3 hours
Parking	Layby on the Hamsterley Road at Wear Bank, opposite the drive to Ashes Farm (Ashes House on map). The layby is situated below power cables spanning the road at this point
Refreshments	Pubs at Wolsingham and Frosterley
Ordnance Survey maps	Landranger 92 (Barnard Castle & surrounding area), Outdoor Leisure 31 (Teesdale)

Too often Weardale is neglected in favour of the more famous Teesdale. This walk may stimulate an interest in its delightful countryside. There are no severe gradients in this stroll, which passes through the pastures of the valley to climb to the grouse moor above. There are spectacular views along and over Weardale from the long-distance path – the Weardale Way – which follows the top of the valley at this point. The return is made on the path that follows the south bank of the river.

Cross the road to the track to Ashes Farm opposite – there is no waymark. Wolsingham looks picturesque from this track. It dips down to cross a stream; Ashes Farm is on the right. Beyond, it continues as a good field track to pass through the farmyard at Towdy Potts.

Turn left after the farmyard **Ⓐ** through a gate onto another, equally pleasing field track. On the right a line of thorn trees shows that the hedgerow is ancient. Frosterley can be seen in the distance beyond them. The track ends at a gap in a stone wall **Ⓑ** with electric lines overhead. Turn left here to follow the wall up the hill towards the small wood at the top.

The footpath swings away eastwards at the bottom of the plantation to meet with a bridleway at a small gate in the stone wall on the left. Do not go through this but turn right and climb through a small patch of gorse to reach the gate at the top of the field by the wood **Ⓒ**.

Go through the gate and turn right onto the broad track that winds over the moor, following the wall that divides it from the pastures below. There are splendid views over Weardale; Stanhope can be seen in the distance. Far ahead, on the skyline, is a clump of trees, known locally as the Elephant Trees. One field before them, go through the gate on the right **Ⓓ** and descend towards Frosterley with the wall on the right.

Almost immediately a circular

sheepfold with fir trees growing within its walls comes into view below. Pass to the right of this, continuing to follow the wall on the right. Having gone through the gate at the bottom of this field, you pass another circular sheepfold, this time on the right. The path joins a track that curves round the hill to a gate in the lower, left-hand corner of the field. The Frosterley quarries are in sight below as the track bears off to the right and away from the village, following the wall on the left. Keep following the track when it turns to the left through a red gate to reach the farm at West Biggins. Do not take the track to the right, which leaves the farmyard, but continue down to cross a bridge. Fork left before Broadwood to reach, and cross, a level-crossing.

If you wish to seek refreshment in Frosterley, carry on over the bridge and turn left along a byway before the main road for a quiet route to the village. Otherwise, turn right **E** before the bridge onto a riverside path.

Keeping strictly to the path, cross the meadow to a footbridge over the Bollihope Burn, which then leads into a short stretch of woodland close to the river.

The footpath continues along the riverbank as it skirts a vast array of caravans on the right. Just before the end of the site the path bends away from the river, passing the managerial bungalow, and then turns left to follow a tarmac driveway, with the railway close to the right.

When the drive bears off to the left to cross the bridge over the Wear, keep straight on along a narrow footpath with the river close to the left. The sound of rushing water heralds a weir, opposite which the path goes through a small gate, across a footbridge and into a long, narrow meadow. Keep to the right-hand side of this, close to the rail-

way. The walking is pleasant here on sheep-cropped turf as it is through a second, even longer meadow.

The river is now some distance to the left. Go over another footbridge into a third narrow meadow, still keeping to the railway side – but do not head for the tempting white gate at the end.

Soon you can see the road bridge over the railway ahead; go up the steps to the road and turn right. The brief climb that follows to return to the starting place is the most taxing that is encountered on this route.

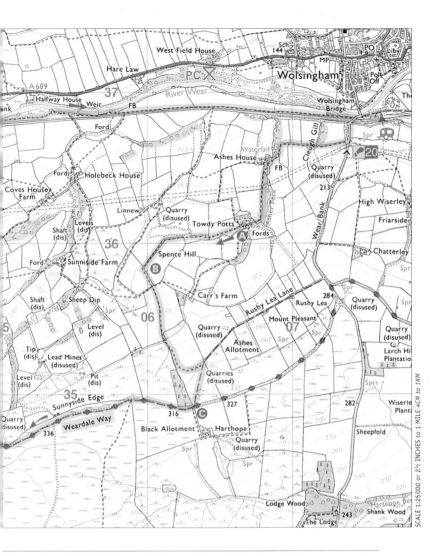

SCALE 1:25000 or 2½ INCHES to 1 MILE 4CM to 1KM

Wolsingham, County Durham

Alston and the South Tyne Valley

Start	Alston Station
Distance	7½ miles (12.1km)
Approximate time	3½ hours
Parking	Alston Station
Refreshments	Café at Alston Station, pubs and cafés at Alston
Ordnance Survey maps	Landranger 86 (Haltwhistle & Brampton, Bewcastle & Alston), Outdoor Leisure 31 (North Pennines – Teesdale & Weardale)

After leaving Alston, the first part of the walk follows the Pennine Way – sometimes across rough, grassy moorland – to the Roman fort of Whitley Castle and on to Kirkhaugh. The return leg is along the South Tyne Trail, a footpath that keeps beside the track of the South Tynedale Railway back to Alston Station. On both legs of the route there are fine views over the valley of the South Tyne to the enveloping stark moorlands.

The former lead-mining town of Alston is situated in the upper reaches of the South Tyne valley and claims to be the highest market town in England. It retains a pleasantly unchanged and 'off the beaten track' air, with steep, cobbled streets and narrow alleys radiating from the Market Square. The imposing Victorian church was built in 1869.

The station served a branch line, opened in 1852 to link Alston with the main Carlisle–Newcastle line at Haltwhistle. It closed in 1976, and since 1983 part of its length has been operated by the narrow-gauge South Tynedale Railway, using a mixture of steam and diesel locomotives.

Begin by walking up to the road and turn right through Alston. Just after bending right to cross the bridge over the South Tyne, turn right by a war memorial and almost immediately right

again Ⓐ along a track through trees, at a Pennine Way sign. Climb a stone stile to emerge from the trees and keep by a wall on the left. Over to the right is a fine view of the town above the east bank of the river. Go through a gate, continue along an enclosed path, passing to the left of a house, climb a stone stile and keep along the right-hand edge of a field, by a wall on the right. After going through the next gate, continue by the wall along the right-hand edges of two fields, go through another gate and, at a Pennine Way sign just ahead, bear left along the left-hand field edge towards a large house, picking up a track.

Go through a gate, follow the track as it bends right at the corner of the buildings and, where it starts to bend right again, bear slightly left across a field, making for a stone stile and

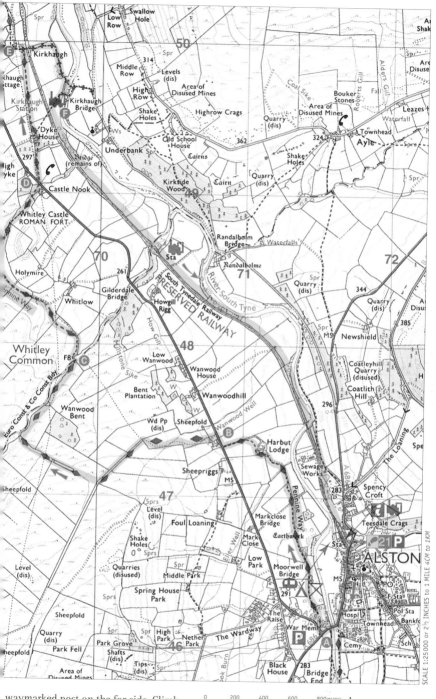

waymarked post on the far side. Climb
the stile and turn left along an enclosed,
tree-lined track to a road. Turn right,
turn left over a stile at a Pennine Way
sign B and head across to go through a
metal gate. Continue steadily uphill

across rough pasture, by a wall on the
left, curving right to climb a stone stile
in the field corner. All around are

extensive views across the bleak moorland of Whitley Common.

Keep ahead across three fields, going through two kissing-gates, and in the third field descend to a gate. Go through and continue downhill to first climb a stone stile and then cross a footbridge over Gilderdale Burn Ⓒ. Climb a stile on the other side, keep ahead to a wall corner and turn right onto a path that continues steadily uphill, by a wall on the right, later veering left to a ladder-stile. After climbing it, bear right to return to the wall, but at a corner do not follow the wall to the right but continue uphill to join a track and keep along it to a ladder-stile.

Climb the stile, keep ahead to go through a metal gate and continue along the track, which curves right, keeping parallel to a wall on the right. Beyond the wall are the striking earthworks of the Roman fort of Whitley Castle, built to guard one of the main routes to Hadrian's Wall. The track heads downhill to join the wall, where you turn right over a ladder-stile. Bear left, head downhill towards farm buildings, above a small burn on the left, and climb a stile. Continue down a narrow path, which bends sharply left to cross a footbridge over the burn and then winds down through trees to climb a stone stile onto a road Ⓓ.

Alston Station on the South Tynedale Railway

Cross over, go through the gate opposite, bear slightly left and walk across a field towards a white cottage. Cross a footbridge and go through a gate, head across a field corner to climb a stile and turn left along the left-hand field edge, passing to the right of a farm. At a wall corner, keep ahead to pass through a gap in the left-hand field corner and continue by the left-hand edge of the next two fields, going through two gates. After the second gate, continue across rough grassland towards the farm buildings at Kirkhaugh, go through a gate and keep ahead to cross a footbridge and reach a Pennine Way sign Ⓔ.

Turn right along a tarmac track – here leaving the Pennine Way – go through a gate under a disused railway bridge and continue downhill along a rough track. The track curves right by a wall and fence on the left and turns left to a gate. Go through and turn right alongside a wall on the right, briefly by the bank of the South Tyne, to a footbridge. Do not cross it but turn right over a stone stile, turn left to follow a path uphill through trees and continue across a field, looking out for a stile in a wire fence by Kirkhaugh Station. Climb it and turn left beside the railway line Ⓕ to join the South Tyne Trail, a footpath that runs beside part of the track of the former Alston–Haltwhistle Railway.

The rest of the walk follows the railway line back to Alston Station, through several gates and both under and over bridges. There are fine views all the way across the South Tyne valley, and the highlights are probably the crossing of first Gilderdale Burn and later the river itself.

Approaching the town of Alston, the route switches to the opposite side of the railway track for the final stretch.

Waskerley Way

Start	Waskerley
Distance	7½ miles (12.1km). Shorter version 5½ miles (8.9km)
Approximate time	4 hours (3 hours for the shorter version)
Parking	Picnic site at Waskerley
Refreshments	Pubs at Castleside
Ordnance Survey maps	Landrangers 87 (Hexham & Haltwhistle) and 88 (Tyneside & Durham), Pathfinder 571, NZ 04/14 (Lanchester)

The trackbeds of disused railways provide many excellent walks in County Durham: this route uses a section of one of the oldest of these. Originally built in 1834 to transport limestone and iron ore from Weardale to Consett, it was later owned by that most famous of railway companies, the Stockton & Darlington. The return from Castleside passes through a variety of terrain. Much of it is on field paths, but quiet lanes, moorland and woodland tracks are used as well. A shorter version is also offered.

It seems incredible today that the lofty, remote moorland hamlet of Waskerley was once a busy railway centre, having a locomotive shed that housed six engines. Only a few buildings survive from its heyday, amongst them the chapel. The line was closed in 1968.

Leave the picnic site and turn left along the old railway track, passing what could have been the engine shed, with heavily buttressed walls, and the chapel. There is a wide view beyond; the Cheviots can be seen on a clear day. Waskerley stands at 1,150ft (350m) above sea-level. There is a planting of conifers in the broad cutting where once there were sidings. Pass a seat Ⓐ thoughtfully sited at an excellent viewpoint and a little further on go through the gate on the left onto the track to Red House, thus cutting off a corner. The Waskerley Way officially goes on to Burnhill Junction, where it

joined a later railway going to Crook and Darlington; if you take this longer route you would turn sharply left to reach Red House.

Turn left at Red House onto the Waskerley Way again. On a windy day it may be wise to walk at the bottom of the deep cutting but then you miss the view that you can enjoy from the path along the top. Over to the left is Nanny Mayer's Incline, where full trucks loaded with ore or limestone were used to haul empty ones back up to Waskerley. Mrs Mayer kept a pub close by.

The deep cutting is followed by a broad, high embankment fringed with rowans. After a bridge the old course of the line from the incline joins from the left. A little distance after, you will come to the White Hall picnic place Ⓑ where the road crosses the track. Turn left onto the road here and after 400 yds (366m) turn right over a stile onto a

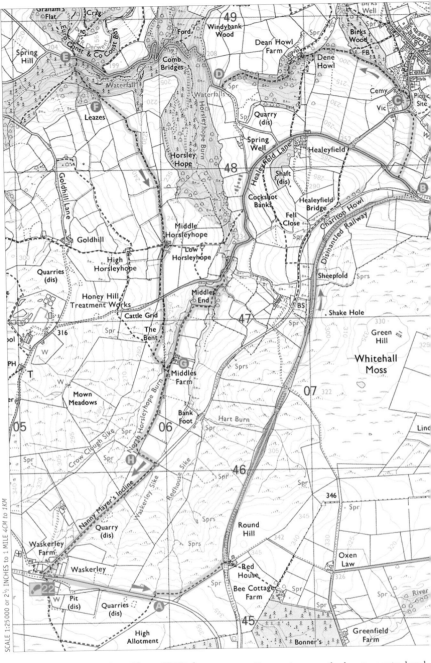

footpath towards Castleside.

The shorter version of this route entails following the road (Healeyfield Lane) to rejoin the longer route at Middles Farm **G**

To continue on the longer route, head to the left of a ruined building to find a gap in the wire fence and then drop to the road at Watergate Burn. Follow the road uphill for a few yards before taking a narrow footpath on the left **C** leading to a lovely wooded valley. After this, pass through the gate and walk along the edge of the field with a fence on the right. A track leads on past Dene Howl Farm on the right and then climbs a narrow, steep-sided and dry valley. This resembles Devon more than Durham.

Turn right at the road **D** and descend a steep hill, twisting down to Comb Bridges; look for footpaths to cut off hairpin bends.

Climb the lane on the other side of the bridge. Soon a ridge is reached – a narrow neck of land with woods dropping away on both sides, separating the valley of the River Derwent from that of the Hisehope Burn. Look for the point where a footpath crosses the road **E** and take the path on the left, which plunges straight down the side of the valley to a footbridge at the bottom. On the other side of the stream, timber operations have obliterated the footpath.

Climb straight over the rough ground as best you can to the fence at the top. If it is a wooden fence, turn to the left to find the point where it joins another wire fence (a wire fence goes up the hillside at right-angles to both). The path climbs on the left side of the ascending fence, bearing to the left through the trees near the top to reach a pair of ancient wicket-gates, which take the path into a field **F**.

Cross this field to a red gate by a length of stone wall. Go through this gate and keep the wall, and then a steep bank, on the left through the field. The path is now following a track going towards Middle Horsleyhope.

Pass through the farmyard and walk down the farm track to the road. Cross over this to another farm track, leading to Middles Farm **G**. Note that the official right-of-way detours to the right after the stream, rejoining close to the farm. There is little sign of this path on the ground.

After the hairpin bends, keep straight on, away from the farm towards a clump of pines. Turn right, following the wall on the left. Waskerley comes into view ahead. Keep the wall on the left past three fields until you come to a patched-up gate in this wall **H** with a ruined building beyond. (Was this once Nanny Mayer's pub?) Use this short track to reach the incline and climb this interesting relic of a bygone age to reach Waskerley. ●

The path from Healeyfield Lane to Castleside

Appleby, Rutter Force and the River Eden

Start	Appleby-in-Westmorland
Distance	8½ miles (13.7km)
Approximate time	4½ hours
Parking	Appleby
Refreshments	Pubs and cafés at Appleby, pub at Hoff, café at Rutter Force, pub at Great Ormside
Ordnance Survey maps	Landranger 91 (Appleby-in-Westmorland), Outdoor Leisure 19 (Howgill Fells & Upper Eden Valley)

Take your time over this walk for there is plenty of interest and variety and much fine scenery to enjoy. It starts in an attractive riverside town, complete with medieval church and castle, and passes by an impressive waterfall to a quiet and remote village with an old church overlooking the River Eden. Finally comes a delightful ramble mostly along the edge of tree-lined meadows beside the lovely River Eden.

Appleby was the county town of Westmorland and 'in-Westmorland' was added to it as a way of perpetuating the name of the county after the local government changes of 1974 abolished it. The town lies within a horseshoe bend of the River Eden and has a fine, wide main street – Boroughgate – that slopes up from the medieval church at the bottom to the Norman castle at the top, lined by verges and old cottages. Leading off from Boroughgate is the Hospital of St Anne, an attractive courtyard of almshouses founded in 1651 by Lady Anne Clifford, who also restored the nearby castle.

Start at the bottom of Boroughgate and, with your back to the church, walk up it towards the castle and turn right in front of the castle gates. The road curves left and heads downhill. Turn right along the road signposted to Colby and by the side of a building and at a public footpath sign to Bandley Bridge, turn left **A** along a tarmac drive to a ladder-stile. Climb it, walk along the left-hand edge of a field, climb a stile in the corner and turn right along a track.

Turn left over a ladder-stile, continue gently uphill along the left-hand field edge, climb another ladder-stile and turn right onto an enclosed track. In front of a gate, turn left over a stile, walk along the right-hand field edge and look out for where you turn right over a ladder-stile. Head diagonally across a field to climb a waymarked stile on the far side and continue in the same direction across the next field, heading downhill and making for the bottom right-hand corner, where you pass through a gap in a hedgebank.

Just beyond that, turn right over a ladder-stile, turn left alongside Hoff

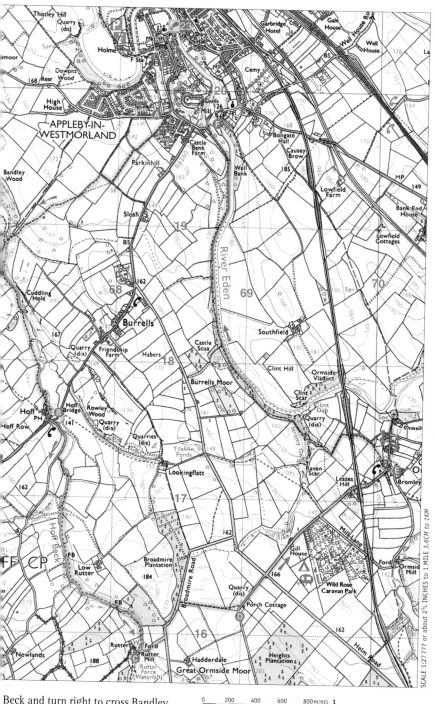

Beck and turn right to cross Bandley Bridge over it. Climb a stile, turn left and walk across to a kissing-gate. Go through and head uphill – not along the sunken track but the path to the left of it – and climb another stile at the top.

Now keep by Hoff Beck across a succession of fields, negotiating a series of gates and stiles and keeping more or less in a straight line, thus cutting across field corners rather than following all the meanders of the beck. Finally bear slightly right away from the beck towards a farm, go through a gate into the farmyard and turn left along a track to a road in the hamlet of Hoff **B**.

Take the narrow lane ahead, signposted to Oakbeck and Drybeck, and at a public footpath sign to Rutter Force and Haybanks turn left through a gate and walk along a hedge-lined track, which bends right alongside Hoff Beck again. Go through a gate, keep beside the beck and turn left to cross a footbridge over it. Turn right to walk by the left bank of the beck – along the edge of meadows and over a succession of stiles – eventually turning right over a footbridge and turning left to continue along the right bank. After climbing a stile, keep ahead towards Rutter Force, passing through a wall gap to reach it **C**.

Turn left over a footbridge – this is where you get the best view of the fall – and walk along a lane up to a T-junction. Turn left and at a public footpath sign to Ormside, turn right over a stile and head gently uphill along the right-hand field edge. After climbing a stile on the brow, a grand view unfolds ahead of the impressive peaks of the North Pennines. Keep ahead over another stile and bear left across the next field to climb a stile onto a lane in front of a cottage **D**. Turn left and follow the switchback lane – over a crossroads and under a railway bridge – into the small village of Great Ormside.

Continue through the village to the hall, originally a 14th-century peel tower, and the church at the far end. The sturdy Norman church with a low saddleback tower, almost fortress-like, occupies a fine position overlooking the Eden and Ormside Viaduct. The site is an ancient one, possibly a Viking burial ground.

Retrace your steps through the village and at a public footpath sign to Appleby, turn right over a stile **E** and walk along a path that curves left to another stile. After climbing that, bear slightly right across the lower slopes of a field – later by a wire fence on the right – and go through a gate onto a track. Keep ahead along the enclosed track which heads gently uphill and, immediately after passing under a railway bridge, climb the ladder-stile in front, at a public footpath sign 'Appleby via River Eden'. Walk along the left-hand field edge, bending left to continue along a wide, grassy, hedge-lined track that gently descends to pass between gateposts.

Turn right along the right-hand edge of the field, heading down to climb a stile, and continue through trees down to a footbridge. Turn left over it, follow a path uphill and around a right bend and climb a stile in the fence on the right. Now the fence is on your left as you climb another stile and continue along the top inside edge of sloping woodland. Look out for where a waymarked post directs you to turn right down steps to the river, bear left and continue along the bottom inside edge of the trees, soon joining the riverbank.

Now follows a delightful walk mostly along the edge of tree-lined meadows beside the River Eden back to Appleby, climbing a series of stiles on the way.

Eventually you bear slightly left away from the river to climb a stile and walk along a narrow path and through a kissing-gate onto a lane **F**. Turn left uphill, keep ahead along a road, picking up the outward route, and turn left down Boroughgate to return to the start.

Barnard Castle, Cotherstone and the River Tees

Start	Barnard Castle
Distance	8½ miles (13.7km)
Approximate time	4½ hours
Parking	Barnard Castle
Refreshments	Pubs and cafés at Barnard Castle, pubs at Cotherstone
Ordnance Survey maps	Landranger 92 (Barnard Castle & surrounding area), Outdoor Leisure 31 (North Pennines – Teesdale & Weardale)

Almost the whole of this walk is along the well-waymarked Teesdale Way. The outward route keeps above the south bank of the river to the attractive village of Cotherstone and crosses the Tees a little further on. The return leg is above the north side and, after descending the steep wooded banks, the last 1½ miles (2.4km) is beside the river itself, a delightful and relaxing finale. Although quite a lengthy and undulating route, there is no particularly steep or difficult climbing. With magnificent views up and down Teesdale, beautiful woodland and grand riverside walking, it is worth taking plenty of time over this outstanding and highly memorable walk.

Barnard Castle occupies a fine position above the River Tees, its main street, lined by dignified stone buildings, sloping down to the old bridge over the river. In the town centre stands the 18th-century Market Cross, once used for the selling of dairy produce, hence its alternative name of Butter Cross. Nearby is the large medieval church, founded around the same time as the castle. It retains some Norman work, especially in the nave, but was enlarged and remodelled over the succeeding centuries, particularly in the 15th century under Richard, Duke of Gloucester, later Richard III.

The town gets its name from the castle built by Bernard de Baliol in the 12th century. Its ruins, dominated by a circular tower, crown a long ridge above the Tees and look particularly impressive when seen from the river. On the east side of the town is the massive Bowes Museum, built in the 19th century in the style of a French château by John and Josephine Bowes. It is well worth a visit and houses a fine collection of paintings, furniture, costume and ceramics.

The walk begins in the town centre by the Market Cross. Walk through the Market Place and continue along Horse Market to the bottom of Galgate. Turn left here along a tarmac drive, passing to the right of the castle entrance, and at a public footpath sign 'Riverside

Walk and Cotherstone' a little further on, the drive bears right and heads downhill, bending first to the left and then to the right, to continue beside the River Tees.

Turn left to cross Deepdale Aqueduct over the river **A**, built in 1893 to carry water from the reservoirs in Baldersdale – and pause to admire the classic view of Barnard Castle rising above the Tees. Turn right along a road, almost immediately turn right again, at public bridleway and Teesdale Way signs, go through a gate and walk along a drive to a stile. Climb it, keep along a track beside the river and, after going through a gate, continue through Pecknell Wood, crossing a bridge over a beck. At a waymarked post – where the track curves left – bear right onto a narrow path to climb a stile and keep ahead gently uphill through trees. Ascend steps by a remaining arch of the demolished Tees Viaduct, built in 1861, and bear left along the disused railway track.

Ignore the stile ahead and climb the waymarked one to the right of it **B**. Walk along the right-hand edge of steeply sloping woodland and, after about 100 yds (91m), climb a stile in a fence and continue, now by a fence and hedge on the left. Climb a stile in the field corner, walk along a track towards a farm but before reaching it turn left onto another track, keeping by a wire fence on the right. Turn right at a fence corner, keep along the right-hand field edge towards trees and turn left to continue along the right-hand edge to a stile. Climb it, keep ahead down steps to cross a footbridge, ascend steps to climb

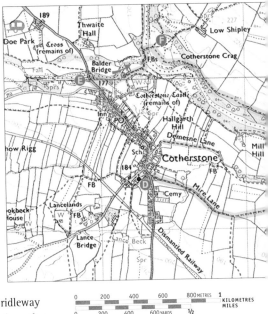

a stile and turn right along the right-hand edge of a field. In the corner, turn left to continue along the field edge and in the next corner follow the field edge to the left again and descend steps to cross another footbridge. Climb more steps, keep along the right-hand edge of a field, climb a stile, turn right along the right-hand edge of the next field and turn left in the corner to continue along its right-hand edge.

Turn right over a stile, head downhill through woodland to climb another one and bear right to cross a footbridge over a beck. Just beyond this bridge, bear left onto an uphill track, climb a stile, keep ahead across a field and climb a stile in the far corner to the right of a barn. Continue by the right-hand edge of the next field, bearing right to climb a stile in a wire fence, and keep by the right-hand field edge towards a farm. Do not go through the gate in the field corner but turn left **C** along a stony track in front of the farmhouse, go through a gate and continue in a straight line across fields, bearing slightly right to a gate. Go through and walk along a

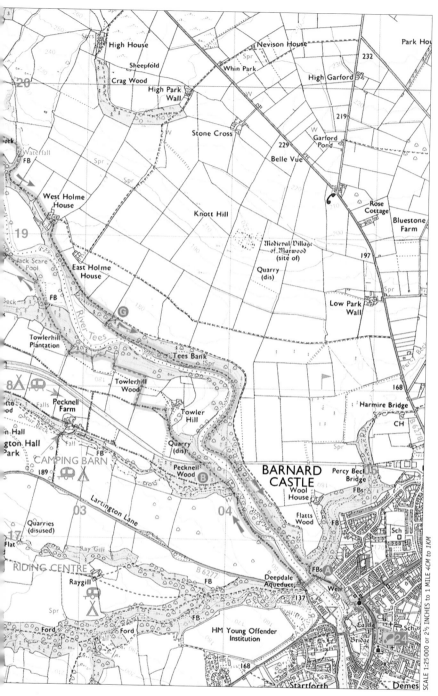

hedge-lined track (Mire Lane) to emerge onto a road in Cotherstone **D**, an attractive village with an imposing 19th-century church.

Turn right through the village, passing to the left of a triangular green. Just

before reaching the bridge over the River Balder, turn right **E** through a gate in a wall, descend steps and follow a well-waymarked path beside the river. The path soon bears right to continue, by a hedge on the left and below an embankment on the right, to a gate. Go through and turn left along a tarmac track, which bears right and continues down to the River Tees. At a Teesdale Way post, turn left to cross a footbridge over the Balder – by its confluence with the Tees – continue by the Tees and turn right to cross a footbridge over it.

Turn right **F**, head across a meadow and on the far side cross footbridge over a small beck and follow a path into riverside woods. The path climbs steeply to a stile. Climb it, walk along the top inside edge of the woodland, by a wall on the left, climb a stone stile in that wall and continue – now with the wall on the right – to a stile in the field corner. After climbing that, follow a switchback route along the right-hand edge of a field, go through a gate, continue along the right-hand edge of the next field but, where the wall bears right, keep straight ahead, making for a stone stile in the wall on the far side.

Climb it, turn right down a steep embankment to cross a footbridge over a beck and turn right onto a path above the beck, which heads up to keep by a wire fence on the left. The path bends left to continue once more along the top edge of steeply sloping riverside woods. Climb a stile, walk along a track to climb another one and continue towards a farm. After climbing the next stile, keep ahead to pass in front of the farmhouse and climb a ladder-stile. Bear right and continue along the top edge of the woods again, climbing a succession of stiles, as far as a way-marked gate in a fence on the right **G**.

Go through the gate, head steeply downhill towards the river and go through another gate at the bottom. Turn left alongside a wall and after going through a gate in the corner of a meadow, the remainder of the walk is an undulating and attractive route along the bottom edge of woodland, either beside or above the River Tees. Just after crossing a footbridge over a beck, you reach Deepdale Aqueduct **A** and from here you retrace your steps to the start.

Barnard Castle rising above the River Tees.

High and Low Force

Start	Bowlees Visitor Centre, near Middleton-in-Teesdale
Distance	8½ miles (13.7km)
Approximate time	4½ hours
Parking	Car park at the visitor centre on the eastern side of Bow Lee Beck
Refreshments	None on the route but a pub at Langdon Beck
Ordnance Survey maps	Landrangers 91 (Appleby-in-Westmorland) or 92 (Barnard Castle & surrounding area), Outdoor Leisure 31 (Teesdale)

The path by the River Tees upstream from Low to High Force is one of the best-known footpaths in the north. This is understandable for it not only provides the best viewpoint for one of the most spectacular British waterfalls but is also a superb riverside walk in itself. The return is on little-used paths and byways along the north side of the valley and is hardly less enjoyable. If a more taxing route is needed, this can be combined with Walk 18 to take in another famous cascade – Cauldron Snout. This would cover a distance of about 17 miles (27km).

From Bowlees car park, cross the bridge to the visitor centre, which contains an exhibition illustrating the natural and human history of the area. From here go down the short lane to reach the main road and cross it to a footpath opposite the telephone-box. Holwick Lodge is the large house on the other side of the valley. The footpath leads across fields to woods and then descends to Wynch Bridge Ⓐ, a lovely suspension bridge spanning a ravine just below the cataract of Low Force. This series of falls is more beautiful than High Force and offers photographers the opportunity of a wider range of viewpoints.

Cross the bridge and turn right to follow the river upstream past the waterfalls. Try to avoid damaging the grassy path, which is assaulted by many thousands of feet each summer. It is reseeded in autumn, so be careful of these bare patches. Dippers are amongst the species of birds that get their living on this stretch of the Tees.

After the bridge that takes a track up to Holwick Head House, climb a reconstituted path to reach the gate into Upper Teesdale Nature Reserve. A good path threads past enormous juniper bushes that resemble the shape of Irish yews; this is the most extensive juniper wood in England. Take the path that forks to the right to view High Force. Most people see the magnificent fall from the opposite side, but this spot shows it better, in a setting of wild hills. With a drop of 70ft (24m) it is England's grandest waterfall.

Continuing westwards on the Tees-side Path, the scenery is marred by the large quarry on the north side of the river. Red flags warn of blasting. If you look away from the quarry you see the beautiful waterfall of Bleabeck Force on the left as a stream tumbles down from Whiteholm Bank. There are footbridges over a couple of sizeable streams and stepping-stones over a third before the path is led up the boggy side of Bracken Rigg by a causeway of planks. Near the top there is a good view on the right over the valley to the white cottages of Forest-in-Teesdale.

There is a Pennine Way signpost a little further on **B**. A route to Cauldron Snout – over Thistle Green to Birkdale – looks inviting on the left, however, our path is to the right, descending over rough rock to Cronkley Farm. Go

through the gate with the acorn emblem of the Pennine Way on it and follow the wall on the right past the farm. Walk down the farm track to the river and cross the bridge. Turn left **C** onto a riverside path through a meadow. Opposite Wheysike House on the other side of the Tees, the narrow path runs under a low cliff close to the river over rocks that are slippery when wet. The Pennine Way leaves our route at Saur Hill Bridge, where we turn right, following the sign along the track towards the youth hostel.

Cross straight over the road and climb the track to East Underhurth. Go through the gate into the farmyard **D** and turn right, passing through another

gate towards the next farm, Hodge Hall. This is a charming building, characteristic of Upper Teesdale, with a byre at the end. Cross the field in front of the farm diagonally to a ladder over the wall in its lower, right-hand corner. Cross the next field to the farmyard of Hanging Shaw. After the two houses here, follow the farm drive down towards the main road. Before you reach it, turn left at the school 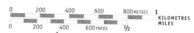.

After the cottage called 'The Dale' it looks as though you are walking to a dead-end of undergrowth. Persevere to a stile at the end of this and climb it into a sunken lane running beside the wall on the right, which was once the main road. Pass in front of Dale Cottage to join a made-up road. There is an Ebenezer Methodist chapel on the left, dating from 1880. Carry straight on when the road bears right to a farm. There are still traces of an ancient trackway here with a slight embankment on the left (the wall is on the right). Go through a black gate – there is a cottage on the right, East Moor Riggs – and then two more gates to head for the farmhouse with the black shed below (the one on the right, not a similar one – Birch Bush – further up on the left). Go to the left of the former cottage, which is Birch Rigg, to reach the road and turn right.

After ½ mile (800m), fork left off this road 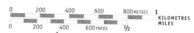 to Dirt Pitt – a misnomer for a charming spot with its stream, waterfall and picturesque cottage. The name is actually a corruption of Deer Peth, a reference to an ancient hunting-forest. Beyond here the lane becomes a track, dipping down to another stream. This is glorious countryside, with views through 360°. Ash Hill is passed on the right, and the woods surrounding Bowlees come into view. The final part of the walk is through delightful meadowland (please remember to shut the gates), dipping down to reach the visitor centre, which was the starting point.

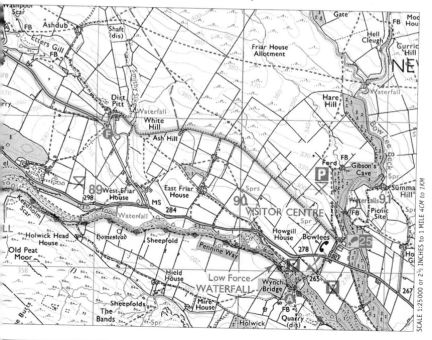

High Cup Nick

Start	Dufton
Distance	8 miles (12.9km)
Approximate time	4 hours
Parking	Dufton
Refreshments	Pub at Dufton, also snacks and soft drinks at Dufton post office
Ordnance Survey maps	Landranger 91 (Appleby-in-Westmorland), Outdoor Leisure 19 (Howgill Fells & Upper Eden Valley) or 31 (North Pennines – Teesdale & Weardale)

The deep, narrow, perfectly U-shaped and almost geometrical chasm of High Cup Gill is one of the great natural wonders of the Pennines. This 'there and back' walk takes you along the Pennine Way to High Cup Nick at the head of the chasm. On the descent back to Dufton, there are superb views ahead all the while across the Eden valley to the Lakeland fells on the horizon. The climb is a steady and unremitting one, with no steep or strenuous sections, along generally clear and well-defined tracks but there is some rough walking on the higher parts, and this walk should not be attempted in bad weather, especially misty conditions, unless experienced in walking in such conditions and able to navigate by using a compass.

For details of Dufton, see Walk 12.

Turn right out of the car park, follow the road around left- and right-hand bends out of the village and, after crossing a bridge over a beck, turn left onto a tarmac track, at a Pennine Way sign to High Cup Nick Ⓐ. Now begins a lengthy but easy and gradual climb.

The track heads gently uphill in a straight line to a gate. Go through and

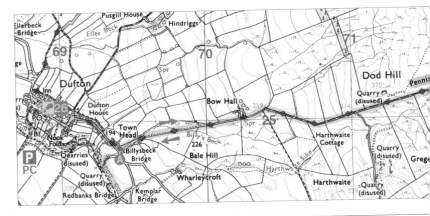

bear right to continue uphill along a broad, walled and rough track. Keep along the left-hand, upper track at a fork and go through three more gates. After the third one, you almost immediately climb a stile, and the way continues through an increasingly wilder and rockier landscape, with the route marked by cairns. Later the path keeps along the rim of High Cup Gill and there are grand views ahead looking towards the head of the chasm, with the bare moorlands beyond.

At a fork, take the left-hand, upper path – there is a waymarked stone here – continuing across rocks, fording several becks and finally walking along a smooth, flat, grassy path to reach High Cup Nick . This is one of the most dramatic viewpoints on the whole of the Pennine Way, looking down the length of the steep, narrow and almost perfectly symmetrical U-shaped valley.

From here, retrace your steps to the start. On the long descent there are

Nigh Cup Nick

superb views ahead all the while, looking across the Eden valley to the line of the Lakeland fells on the horizon, with the conically shaped Dufton Pike nearer at hand and the village nestling below. ●

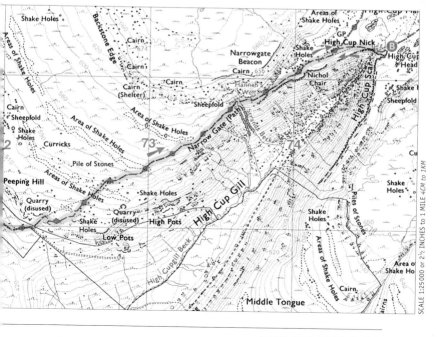

Crosthwaite Common, Rake Gill and Holwick

Start	Middleton-in-Teesdale
Distance	9½miles (15.3km)
Approximate time	4½ hours
Parking	Middleton-in-Teesdale (Hill Terrace is the most convenient)
Refreshments	Pubs and cafés at Middleton, Strathmore Arms at Holwick (children welcome)
Ordnance Survey maps	Landrangers 91 (Appleby-in-Westmorland) or 92 (Barnard Castle & surrounding area), Outdoor Leisure 31 (Teesdale)

The triangular shape of this route divides, predictably, into three sections. The outward stretch is along the Pennine Way out of Middleton, which provides good walking across pastures with excellent views over Teesdale and then Lunedale, with its man-made lakes. The path turns off to the north-west on a bridleway – sometimes quite difficult to follow on the ground – over grouse moors to reach Holwick; during the grouse-shooting season (12 August–10 December), check access with the local tourist information centre in Barnard Castle (tel. 01833 690909). From here the way back is straightforward, following the riverside path – the Pennine Way again – by the River Tees. It would be as well to bring a compass on this walk.

Cross the bridge at Middleton-in-Teesdale, following the road to Brough and Scotch Corner. Pass the livestock mart and, where the Holwick road goes off the main road to the right, take this turn and immediately look for a bridle-way on the left **Ⓐ**. Go through the gate to walk up the hill on this track. The view of the small town in its lovely valley is outstanding and improves as you get higher.

After a green gate, bear to the right away from the wall, heading towards a flat-topped hill. As you climb there is a distinctive clump of trees on top of the

hill to your left, which marks the site of Kirkcarrion, a Bronze Age burial ground. You will be walking up a path on the left-hand side of a gully, heading towards a gate. After the gate **Ⓑ**, fork to the right, making for the flat-topped hill. The path skirts to the left of its summit, where there is a helpful cairn to guide the way.

Go through the gate in the corner of the pasture at the top. There is a yellow waymark on the next gate. Turn right after this to another gate, which has distinctive white-painted steps taking the path over the wall to its left. Now

Middleton-in-Teesdale

follow the path towards a post bearing a white flash, which stands by a small cairn. From here the view opens up over Lunedale and the reservoirs. Follow the yellow waymark, bearing right towards Selset Reservoir.

Beyond the next gate a grassy track leads past a byre. Cross a stone stile by a gate and head for the farm in the distance ahead (Cornset). After another gate the path descends to a track that passes through a gateway with a yellow waymark. Go down this track for 50 yds (46m) and then bear off it to the right through a gateway heading for Wythes Hill Farm. Cross a stream by stepping-stones and continue down to ford the Carl Beck. Just before the farm, where the track bears left , go through a gate on the right. This has a figure 8 painted on the stone gatepost.

Turn left to follow the wall on the left. The Carl Beck is now on the right. After a gate, the wall you have been following bears off to the left. Here the track is vague but by walking in the same direction – with Cornset ahead, but to the right, two fields distant – you will approach another wall on the right-hand side. There should be a small

stream on the left where the track passes through a red gate onto what looks like the open moor. However, there is still another gate ahead, which you reach by walking with the fence to the right.

Now keep Cornset's boundary wall to the right as the path winds along on the left bank of Merry Gill, which it eventually crosses close to a skeletal shed. From here make for stonework ruins and then follow a winding track into the heathery wastes. It climbs steeply at first, heading north-west, but then levels out. A stone wall comes into view on the left, and the path drops down into Rake Gill , a concealed valley with shooting-butts, a shelter and even a privy.

From the shelter, bear left to climb out of the gill. Go through the gate where the track ends and follow the path that passes to the right of a further flat-topped hill. Suddenly, there is a spectacular surprise, Teesdale is revealed below.

Go through a red gate and begin to descend on a reasonably clear, but soggy, path. This is Crooks o' Green Fell; to the left are rocky crags. When you see a wall ahead, strike off to the right, keeping the wall to the left. You should be close to the wall to cross a stream, Easter Beck. After this there is something of a path leading to a gate at the bottom .

Go through the gate and keep on the distinct path that follows a line bisecting the angle between the wall (on the right) and the fence (left). Cross the Rowton Beck and then head for a white-painted stile below. From here the route

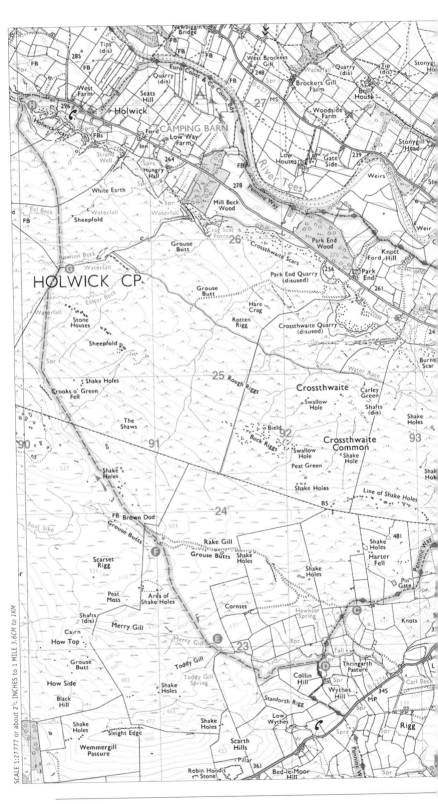

is clearly marked by white posts. It passes a sheepfold and short stretch of high stone walling to reach another white stile. Bear right here, following the white arrow on the stile, passing cairns, to enter a steep and narrow valley, which seems to be leading over the crest of the crag – although this looks like a quarry, in fact it is a natural feature. There is a well-concealed stile here. One might be tempted to think that it is a subterfuge for getting rid of ramblers, but there is a way down, though it is a steep scramble, with the stream to the left. At the bottom, cross the stream and climb the steep bank to turn right **H** onto the track to Holwick.

The pub in Holwick, the Strathmore Arms, lies 400 yds (366m) beyond the point in the village where a path to the left, about 100 yds (91m) past the telephone-box, takes the route down to the River Tees and then onward into Middleton. A stile is thoughtfully placed to avoid the morass at the end of the first field. There is a white-painted stile at the bottom of the next one, but the path does not cross this. Instead, it goes through one in the wall on the right to reach the riverbank by a footbridge. Do not cross this but turn right, following the riverside path eastwards.

There seems to be an endless succession of stiles on this path, which follows the river's course for much of the way through the meadows. It cuts across three of the more extreme meanders as it approaches Middleton and for a short distance follows a sunken lane, which has an ancient feel to it. The path finally leaves the riverside to join a farm track leading past the livestock mart to reach the main road. Turn left here to cross the bridge and return to Middleton.

Bowes Moor

Start	Bowes
Distance	10½ miles (16.9km)
Approximate time	5½ hours
Parking	Bowes, Village Hall car park
Refreshments	Pub at Bowes
Ordnance Survey maps	Landranger 92 (Barnard Castle & surrounding area), Outdoor Leisure 31 (North Pennines – Teesdale & Weardale)

On many parts of this walk there are seemingly endless vistas across wild, open and often bleak moorland. After an initial opening stretch by the delightful River Greta, the route continues along the Pennine Way over Bowes Moor, a particularly valuable and extensive area of heather moorland. A magnificent scenic walk along a ridge leads to an alternative route of the Pennine Way and this is followed across the moor and finally along a lane back to the start. Parts of the route are on faint paths – on one stretch there is no visible path at all – and there is much rough moorland walking. Therefore it is not recommended in bad weather, especially in the winter or in mist, unless you are experienced in walking in this terrain in such conditions and able to navigate by using a compass.

Bowes Castle guards the eastern end of the Stainmore route across the Pennines and, like its counterpart at Brough, which guards the western end, it stands within the earthworks of a Roman fort. The massive, square 12th-century keep is one of the largest in the country. Next to it is the small, restored Norman church.

From the car park, take the lane signposted to Gilmonby, which descends to cross a bridge over the River Greta and continues into the hamlet of Gilmonby. Turn right Ⓐ along the lane to Home Farm and West Gates, and this later becomes a rough track that continues past a series of farms and through a

succession of gates, keeping roughly parallel with the River Greta.

Look out for a Pennine Way post where the track bends right to go through a gate to the right of a farm-house. After going through the next gate, turn left off the track alongside the farm buildings, continue across a meadow and turn right to cross a footbridge over the tributary Sleightholme Beck. Keep ahead through a wall gap, continue by a wall on the left above the river, go through a gate and bear slightly left across a field towards a farm. Go through a gate into the farm-yard, turn first right and then almost immediately left between farm

On Bowes Moor

buildings and bear left along a track that bends right to the next farm.

Go through a gate to the right of the farm, turn half-right to head diagonally across a field and over the brow, descend to a footpath post in the bottom corner. Go through a gate, turn right to cross God's Bridge ⒷB, a natural stone arch over the River Greta, and continue uphill along a track, going through another gate and following the winding track up to a wall in front of the A66 embankment. Turn left alongside it, go through a gate, turn right through another and continue through a subway under the road. The track bends right to go through a gate and continues – parallel to the road – to a farm.

At a Pennine Way sign in front of the farm, turn left ⒸC and head uphill across Bowes Moor, initially by a wall on the right. At the wall corner, bear slightly right and follow a cairned and fairly clear path – likely to be muddy – across the bleak and open heathery moorland, later descending to cross a stony track by Bowes Moor and Pennine Way signs. Beyond these cross a footbridge over Deepdale Beck, keep by a wall on the right to go through a gate and head

steadily uphill beside the wall. Climb a stile in a fence, continue by the wall and, on reaching the brow, turn right through a gate ⒹD. The route now continues along a reasonably discernible grassy track along a broad ridge, from which the views over the surrounding expanses of moorland are magnificent. To the left the reservoirs in Baldersdale can be seen.

The track – which later becomes much clearer – continues to a gate in a wire fence but about 20 yds (18m) in front of it, turn right ⒺE and head downhill across rough grass. This is an alternative route of the Pennine Way but at this point there is no visible path. This does not matter; simply head down to first negotiate a boggy area, then bear right and descend steeply again to ford Hazelgill Beck. Climb above the other side, head downhill again towards a farm and turn right alongside Deepdale Beck. There is a ford by the farm but you cross the beck by the stepping-stones a little further on.

On the other side, return to the ford, turn right through a gate, head uphill to the right of the farm and bear right onto a farm track. The track curves left and you keep along it – going through two gates – to a T-junction ⒻF. Turn right, go through a gate, walk along a track towards a farm and, in front of it, turn left through a waymarked gate. Keep by a wall on the right and, at the wall corner, bear right downhill to a fence corner – there is a yellow waymark here – and bear left to continue across the field, heading up to a stone stile just to the left of a wall corner. Climb it, keep in the same direction across the next field, passing to the left of a barn, and climb a stone stile on the far side.

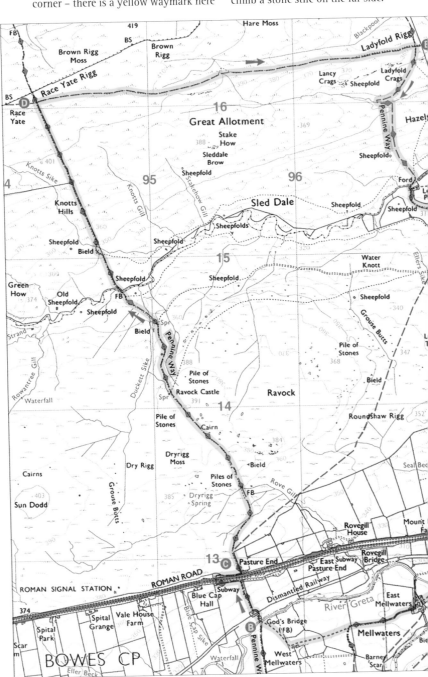

Continue across the next field and, in the far corner, climb a ladder-stile onto a lane **G**. Turn right and follow the lane back to Bowes. Just after the castle comes into view, bear right along a lane towards it, which descends and curves right to cross a bridge over the A66 and then bends left to return to the starting point. ●

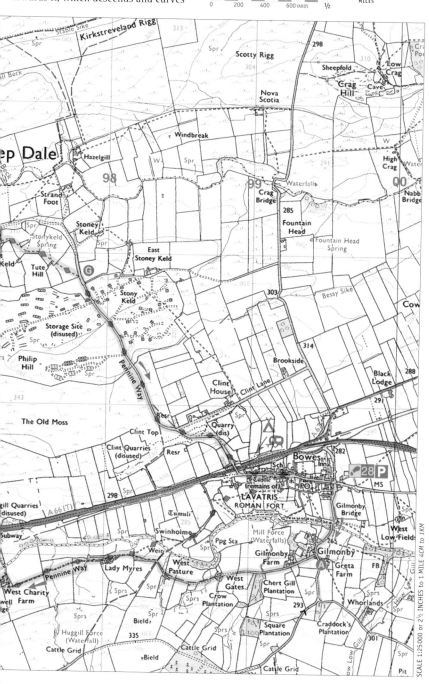

Further Information

The National Trust

Anyone who likes visiting places of natural beauty and/or historic interest has cause to be grateful to the National Trust. Without it, many such places would probably have vanished by now.

It was in response to the pressures on the countryside posed by the relentless march of Victorian industrialisation that the trust was set up in 1895. Its founders, inspired by the common goals of protecting and conserving Britain's national heritage and widening public access to it, were Sir Robert Hunter, Octavia Hill and Canon Rawnsley: respectively a solicitor, a social reformer and a clergyman. The latter was particularly influential. As a canon of Carlisle Cathedral and vicar of Crosthwaite (near Keswick), he was concerned about threats to the Lake District and had already been active in protecting footpaths and promoting public access to open countryside. After the flooding of Thirlmere in 1879 to create a large reservoir, he became increasingly convinced that the only effective way to guarantee protection was outright ownership of land.

The purpose of the National Trust is to preserve areas of natural beauty and sites of historic interest by acquisition, holding them in trust for the nation and making them available for public access and enjoyment. Some of its properties have been acquired through purchase, but many of the Trust's properties have been donated. Nowadays it is not only one of the biggest landowners in the country, but also one of the most active conservation charities, protecting 581,113 acres (253,176 ha) of land, including 555 miles (892km) of coastline, and over 300 historic properties in England, Wales and Northern Ireland. (There is a separate National Trust for Scotland, which was set up in 1931.)

Furthermore, once a piece of land has come under National Trust ownership, it is difficult for its status to be altered. As a result of parliamentary legislation in 1907, the Trust was given the right to declare its property inalienable, so ensuring that in any subsequent dispute it can appeal directly to parliament.

As it works towards its dual aims of conserving areas of attractive countryside and encouraging greater public access (not easy to reconcile in this age of mass tourism), the Trust provides an excellent service for walkers by creating new concessionary paths and waymarked trails, maintaining stiles and foot bridges and combating the ever-increasing problem of footpath erosion.

For details of membership, contact the National Trust at the address on page 95.

The Ramblers' Association

No organisation works more actively to protect and extend the rights and interests of walkers in the countryside than the Ramblers' Association. Its aims are clear: to foster a greater knowledge, love and care of the countryside; to assist in the protection and enhancement of public rights of way and areas of natural beauty; to work for greater public access to the countryside; and to encourage more people to take up rambling as a healthy, recreational leisure activity.

It was founded in 1935 when, following the setting up of a National Council of Ramblers' Federations in 1931, a number of federations earlier formed in London, Manchester, the Midlands and elsewhere came together to create a more effective pressure group, to deal with such problems as the disappearance and obstruction of footpaths, the prevention of access to open mountain and moorland and increasing hostility from landowners. This was the era of the mass trespasses, when there were sometimes violent

The Saxon church at Escomb

confrontations between ramblers and gamekeepers, especially on the moorlands of the Peak District.

Since then the Ramblers' Association has played an influential role in preserving and developing the national footpath network, supporting the creation of national parks and encouraging the designation and waymarking of long-distance routes.

Our freedom to walk in the countryside is precarious and requires constant vigilance. As well as the perennial problems of footpaths being illegally obstructed, disappearing through lack of use or extinguished by housing or road construction, new dangers can spring up at any time.

It is to meet such problems and dangers that the Ramblers' Association exists and represents the interests of all walkers. The address to write to for information on the Ramblers' Association and how to become a member is given on page 95.

Walkers and the Law

The average walker in a national park or other popular walking area, armed with the appropriate Ordnance Survey map, reinforced perhaps by a guidebook giving detailed walking instructions, is unlikely to run into legal difficulties, but it is useful to know something about the law relating to public rights of way. The right to walk over certain parts of the countryside has developed over a long period, and how such rights came into being is a complex subject, too lengthy to be discussed here. The following comments are intended simply as a helpful guide, backed up by the Countryside Access Charter, a concise summary of walkers' rights and obligations drawn up by the Countryside Agency (see page 93).

Basically there are two main kinds of public rights of way: footpaths (for walkers only) and bridleways (for walkers, riders on horseback and pedal cyclists). Footpaths and bridleways are shown by broken green lines on Ordnance Survey Pathfinder and Outdoor Leisure maps and broken red lines on Landranger maps. There is also a third category, called byways: chiefly broad tracks (green lanes) or farm roads, which walkers, riders and cyclists have to share, usually only occasionally, with motor vehicles. Many of these public paths have been in existence for hundreds of years and some even originated as prehistoric trackways

Countryside Access Charter

Your rights of way are:

- public footpaths – on foot only. Sometimes waymarked in yellow
- bridleways – on foot, horseback and pedal cycle. Sometimes waymarked in blue
- byways (usually old roads), most 'roads used as public paths' and, of course, public roads – all traffic has the right of way

Use maps, signs and waymarks to check rights of way. Ordnance Survey Pathfinder and Landranger maps show most public rights of way

On rights of way you can:

- take a pram, pushchair or wheelchair if practicable
- take a dog (on a lead or under close control)
- take a short route round an illegal obstruction or remove it sufficiently to get past

You have a right to go for recreation to:

- public parks and open spaces – on foot
- most commons near older towns and cities – on foot and sometimes on horseback
- private land where the owner has a formal agreement with the local authority

In addition you can use the following by local or established custom or consent, but ask for advice if you are unsure:

- many areas of open country, such as moorland, fell and coastal areas, especially those in the care of the National Trust, and some commons
- some woods and forests, especially those owned by the Forestry Commission
- country parks and picnic sites
- most beaches
- canal towpaths
- some private paths and tracks Consent sometimes extends to horse-riding and cycling

For your information:

- county councils and London boroughs maintain and record rights of way, and register commons
- obstructions, dangerous animals, harassment and misleading signs on rights of way are illegal and you should report them to the county council
- paths across fields can be ploughed, but must normally be reinstated within two weeks
- landowners can require you to leave land to which you have no right of access
- motor vehicles are normally permitted only on roads, byways and some 'roads used as public paths'

and have been in constant use for well over 2,000 years. Ways known as RUPPs (roads used as public paths) still appear on some maps. The legal definition of such byways is ambiguous and they are gradually being reclassified as footpaths, bridleways or byways.

The term 'right of way' means exactly what it says. It gives right of passage over what, in the vast majority of cases, is private land, and you are required to keep to the line of the path and not stray on to the land on either side. If you inadvertently wander off the right of way – either because of faulty map-reading or because the route is not clearly indicated on the ground – you are technically trespassing and the wisest course is to ask the nearest

available person (farmer or fellow walker) to direct you back to the correct route. There are stories about unpleasant confrontations between walkers and farmers at times, but in general most farmers are co-operative when responding to a genuine and polite request for assistance in route-finding.

Obstructions can sometimes be a problem and probably the most common of these is where a path across a field has been ploughed up. It is legal for a farmer to plough up a path provided that he restores it within two weeks, barring exceptionally bad weather. This does not always happen and here the walker is presented with a dilemma: to follow the line of the path, even if this inevitably means treading on crops, or to walk around the edge of the field. The latter course of action often seems the best but this means that you would be trespassing and not keeping to the exact line of the path. In the case of other obstructions which may block a path (illegal fences and locked gates etc), common sense has to be used in order to negotiate them by the easiest method – detour or removal. You should only ever remove as much as is necessary to get through, and if you can easily go round the obstruction without causing any damage, then you should do so. If you have any problems negotiating rights of way, you should report the matter to the rights of way department of the relevant council, which will take action with the landowner concerned.

Apart from rights of way enshrined by law, there are a number of other paths available to walkers. Permissive or concessionary paths have been created where a landowner has given permission for the public to use a particular route across his land. The main problem with these is that, as they have been granted as a concession, there is no legal right to use them and therefore they can be extinguished at any time. In practice, many of these concessionary routes have been established on land owned either by large public bodies such as the Forestry Commission, or by a private one, such as the National Trust, and as these mainly encourage walkers to use their paths, they are unlikely to be closed unless a change of ownership occurs.

Walkers also have free access to country parks (except where requested to keep away from certain areas for ecological reasons, e.g wildlife protection, woodland regeneration, etc), canal towpaths and most beaches. By custom, though not by right, you are generally free to walk across the open and uncultivated higher land of mountain, moorland and fell, but this varies from area to area and from one season to another – grouse moors, for example, will be out of bounds during the breeding and shooting seasons and some open areas are used as Ministry of Defence firing ranges, for which reason access will be restricted. In some areas the situation has been clarified as a result of 'access agreements' between the landowners and either the county council or the national park authority, which clearly define when and where you can walk over such open country.

Further Information

Rutter Force on the River Eden, Cumbria

Safety on the Hills

The hills, mountains and moorlands of Britain, though of modest height compared with those in many other countries, need to be treated with respect. Friendly and inviting in good weather, they can quickly be transformed into wet, misty, windswept and potentially dangerous areas of wilderness in bad weather. Even on an outwardly fine and settled summer day, conditions can rapidly deteriorate. In winter, of course, the weather can be even more erratic and the hours of daylight are much shorter.

Therefore it is advisable to always take both warm and waterproof clothing, sufficient nourishing food, a hot drink, first-aid kit, torch and whistle. Wear suitable footwear, i.e. strong walking boots or shoes that give a good grip over rocky terrain and on slippery slopes. Try to obtain a local weather forecast and bear it in mind before you start. Do not be afraid to abandon your proposed route and return to your starting point in the event of a sudden and unexpected deterioration in the weather. Do not go alone. Allow enough time to finish the walk well before nightfall.

Most of the walks described in this book do not venture into remote wilderness areas and will be safe to do, given due care and respect, at any time of year in all but the most unreasonable weather. Indeed, a crisp, fine winter day often provides perfect walking conditions, with firm ground underfoot and a clarity that is not possible to achieve in the other seasons of the year. A few walks, however, are suitable only for reasonably fit and experienced hill-walkers able to use a compass and should definitely not be tackled by anyone else during the winter months or in bad weather, especially high winds and mist. These are indicated in the general description that precedes each of the walks.

Useful Organisations

Council for the Protection of Rural England
25 Buckingham Palace Road,
London SW1W 0PP. Tel. 020 7976 6433

Countryside Agency
John Dower House, Crescent Place,
Cheltenham, Gloucestershire GL50 3RA.
Tel. 01242 521381

Forestry Commission
Information Branch, 231 Corstorphine Rd,
Edinburgh EH12 7AT.
Tel. 0131 334 0303

High Force

Further Information

Long Distance Walkers' Association
21 Upcroft, Windsor, Berkshire SL4 3NH.
Tel. 01753 866685

National Trust
Membership and general enquiries:
PO Box 39, Bromley, Kent BR1 3XL.
Tel. 020 8315 1111
Northumbria Regional Office:
Scots' Gap, Morpeth,
Northumberland NE61 4EG.
Tel. 01670 774691

Ordnance Survey
Romsey Road, Maybush,
Southampton SO16 4GU.
Tel. 08456 05 05 05 (Lo-call)

Ramblers' Association
1–5 Wandsworth Road, London SW8 2XX.
Tel. 020 7339 8500

Tourist information:
Cumbria Tourist Board
Ashleigh, Holly Road,
Windermere, Cumbria LA23 2AQ.
Tel. 015394 44444
Northumbria Tourist Board
Aykley Heads, Durham DH1 5UX.
Tel. 0191 375 3000
Tourist information centres (*not open all year):
*Alston: 01434 381696
Appleby-in-Westmorland: 017683 51177
Barnard Castle: 01833 690909
Beamish: 0191 370 2533
Bishop Auckland: 01388 604922
*Brampton: 016977 3433
Darlington: 01325 388666
Durham: 0191 384 3720
Kirkby Stephen: 017683 71199
Newcastle upon Tyne: 0191 261 0610/
 230 0030
Stanhope: 01388 527650
South Shields: 0191 454 6612
Sunderland: 0191 553 2000/01/02
Whitley Bay: 0191 200 835

Youth Hostels Association
Trevelyan House, 8 St Stephen's Hill,
St Albans, Hertfordshire AL1 2DY.
Tel. 01727 855215

Weather forecasts:
UK seven-day forecast.
Tel. 0891 333123

 Ordnance Survey Maps of Durham, North Pennines and Tyne & Wear

The area of *Durham, North Pennines and Tyne & Wear* is covered by Ordnance Survey 1:50 000 (1¼ inches to 1 mile or 2cm to 1km) scale Landranger map sheets 86, 87,88, 90, 91, 92, 93, 94. These all-purpose maps are packed with information to help you explore the area and show viewpoints, picnic sites, places of interest and caravan and camping sites.

To examine the *Durham, North Pennines and Tyne & Wear* area in more detail and especially if you are planning walks, Ordnance Survey Outdoor Leisure maps at 1:25 000 (2½ inches to 1 mile or 4cm to 1km) scale are ideal:

 5 English Lakes - North Eastern area
 19 Howgill Fells & Upper Eden Valley
 26 North York Moors – Western area
 27 North York Moors – Eastern area
 30 Yorkshire Dales – Northern & Central
  area
 31 North Pennines – Teesdale & Weardale
 43 Hadrian's Wall

Other maps at 1:25 000 (2½ inches to 1 mile or 4cm to 1km) scale are:

Explorer map: 306 Middlesborough

Pathfinder map sheets:

550	570	580	600
558	571	581	609
561	572	590	610
562	573	599	

To get to the *Durham, North Pennines and Tyne & Wear* area use the Ordnance Survey Great Britain Routeplanner Map (Travelmaster map number 1) at 1:625 000 (1 inch to 10 miles or 1cm to 6.25 km) scale or Travelmaster map 5 (Northern England) at 1:250 000 (1 inch to 4 miles or 1cm to 2.5km) scale.

Ordnance Survey maps and guides are available from most booksellers, stationers and newsagents.

Further Information

Index

Entries in *italic type* refer to illustration